STRONGER

than the Storm

Proven Strategies to Conquer Fear, Discover Strength and Overcome the Unexpected

MICHELE LAINE

STRONGER THAN THE STORM

Proven Strategies to Conquer Fear, Discover Strength and
Overcome the Unexpected

MICHELE LAINE

Inner Strength and Beauty Publishing

Cover and Interior Design: STOKE Publishing
Author Cover Photo Credit: Amy Lopez

If you are a coach or mentor and would like to use this book for a group
coaching session or healing circle, please contact Michele directly for bulk
purchases. Minimum order is required. Thank you! For orders please
email: michele@michelelaine.com

Disclaimer
The author of this book does not dispense medical advice or prescribe the
use of any technique as a form of treatment for physical, emotional, or
medical problems without a physician's advice, either directly or indirectly.
The author's intent is to provide general information to individuals who are
taking positive steps in their lives for emotional and spiritual well-being. If
you use any information in this book for yourself, the author and the
publisher assume no responsibility for your actions.

Find the free resources at:
https://www.michelelaine.com/resource-toolkit

Contents

The Power of a Gratitude Shift

You cannot change your past but you can adopt a fresh
perspective in today's busy and stress-inducing world.
Discover the life-changing effects of making a gratitude shift.
It's proven to benefit both your mental and physical health.

I am grateful for...

daily devotion toward the
embodiment of new habits

I am grateful for...

finding freedom through the
practice of forgiveness

**To grab my *Gratitude Card Experience*, visit
www.michelelaine.com/resource-toolkit**

I learned firsthand that GRATITUDE was my superpower. It allowed me to cultivate more peace and ease in my mind-body and retrain my focus toward a higher perspective available even as chaos ensued.

I would like to invite you to a chance to play with gratitude through a printable playing card experience.

Again, **to grab my *Gratitude Card Experience*, visit www.michelelaine.com/resource-toolkit**

Dedication

Sarah Fragoso, Traci Corbett, & Rina Thoma

*I wouldn't be the person I am today without the influence you have
had on my life. Each of you played a huge part in helping me gain
the skills and confidence necessary to write this book. Your constant
inspiration and friendship provided me the courage I needed
throughout the entire process. Thank you for all of your love and
support. and being a catalyst for growth at this time of my life.*

Introduction

What happens when you lose everything? Can you rebuild and come out stronger? Will your relationships withstand the devastation of hitting rock bottom and losing everything?

As our storm settled in, these were the questions burning inside me, as I'm sure they'd be the same burning within those of you experiencing such a loss.

In this book, I'll not only share my story of how I prevailed through our toughest time of life, but how I came out stronger and more determined to create a new life, full of passions. How my husband and I reinvented ourselves and created new careers.

It's never too late to go for a dream or make a change in your life. You can reinvent yourself, build a new career and maintain a positive outlook on life, at any age—even when it feels your world is collapsing around you.

Part two of this book ends with a Survivor's Toolkit, providing strategies to not only change perspective and focus on passions during the tumultuous times, but manage your time and live a healthier life while doing so. New habits that will serve you through life when the storm clouds part and blue skies shine once more.

I'll share with you my strategies and successes for making it through the storm. This book is for people who've suffered from storms in life, or for those who want to be prepared when their storms come rolling in. Those who wish to reinvent themselves, fulfill their dreams, and take optimum care of themselves. Those who get up each day doing their best to keep a positive outlook on life during this time of stress, uncertainty and fear. Live each day being truly proud of yourself and all you've accomplished.

I'll give you my expertise from not only living through and surviving my storm, but coming out stronger on the other end. I created the toolkit from tried and true strategies during the most stressful time in my life. Strategies I continue to use everyday. These tools can provide steps you can implement right away to create new habits, prioritize yourself and begin living the life you want. Whether you're currently in a storm of your own or not, I know you can do it. If I made these changes, you can do it too!

My story will inspire you to survive your storm. It will inspire you to make the necessary changes in your life and not give up hope when all feels lost. Learn how to face your fears by getting out of your comfort zone and open doors you've never imagined. Learn to go for your dreams, no matter how big or small they may be. To keep moving forward, making choices and decisions, not excuses.

Through my experience, you'll learn how simple it is to follow your own heart with newfound strength and take action to move past the familiar and comfortable.

I promise, by the time you reach the last page, you too will be empowered to make changes in your life. Changes that will help you live healthier and ride through your storm. You'll be inspired to take control of your life, your destiny and your dreams. Make choices that lead you to exactly where you were meant to be in life.

Why wait?

By reading this book, each chapter will unlock insight as you strive to make change. The tips and tools in this book have been proven to create long lasting results. As you keep reading, you'll learn to recognize you have the power to take action today, stop making excuses, start something new that brings you happiness and contentment and create the future you desire.

Take control of your life now, live your dreams and enjoy the ride.

Your journey begins with a turn of the page. See you on the inside.

PART I
The Unexpected Storm

ONE

My Story

Storms are normal parts of weather patterns. Some days are sunny, other days aren't—but that's life. There are big storms and little storms, and even many types of storms, from thunderstorms to hurricanes.

We like to predict when these storms are going to happen so we are ready for them. The meteorologist on TV tells us a storm is coming before it even arrives, and we know that they will end eventually. We can feel safe knowing that the storms will always pass. We come to expect them, especially during certain times of year and in certain parts of the world.

But what if a storm were to enter your life totally out of the blue, and completely tear your life apart? A storm the likes of which you had never seen or expected?

That is what happened to me and my family. We had a good life, full of many blue skies. And then suddenly, an unexpected, category 10 life storm came in and took everything away.

Throughout the tumultuous winds and rains of my storm, I wondered if we would pull through. I wondered if it would ever end. While I kept hope, I did wonder how in the world we could ever recover.

This is my story.

Our life was self built. My husband Scott and I loved being entrepreneurs. There is something so fulfilling about owning your own business. It's a daily commitment and your business becomes a big part of who you are as a person.

My husband and I both worked hard for decades building our natural stone business. We sold wholesale natural stone products to retail landscaping yards and major building material dealers throughout the United States. Over a lot of years and sacrifice, we eventually had over 50 acres of stone materials at multiple distribution center locations in Oklahoma, Idaho, New York and California to serve our customers from across the nation.

Over the years, we patented custom product lines. We acquired quarries of stone, including a one-of-a-kind product out of Northern Idaho. Always, we wanted to add value to the customer experience; our customers always came first. We were a nationwide leader in our industry. We provided an option to our customers to stock products without purchasing full truckloads of the same type of stone material. We became a one-stop-shop for customers to mix and match their products on truckload purchases. Whatever we could do to make things easier on our customers.

Over time, our business expanded from one parent company into five additional subsidiary companies, including our own trucking company to manage all the shipments. We had lots of ups and downs along the way, and especially many proud moments.

We sacrificed and spent all our time on it. Owning your own business may sound glamorous, but it is hard work. It involves long hours and a lot of sacrifice. You don't just work 8 a.m. to 5 p.m. Monday through Friday—you work every day, all day, not always knowing what the financial outcome will be, but you do it anyway. Twelve hour workdays were a normal part of life. There was always something to take care of. As the business grew, so did the obstacles. So we worked harder and smarter.

We built our business together even through the birth of our first daughter, Sami. It wasn't easy doing both, being vice president of finance and a Mom. We made it work, and even though it was challenging at times, I loved having her near us and accepted that challenge. She spent her days with me in the office until she was old enough to attend preschool.

Combining office work and child care is very demanding because you are always needed at work. The challenge was offsetting naptime and feedings with the demands of managing the office and employees once Sami arrived. Constant timing of getting as much work completed and answering as many questions as possible while she napped. Being fully engaged with her while she was awake and fully engaged with our staff. Out of necessity, I mastered efficiency.

Sometimes Scott and I would switch back and forth taking care of Sami. He would juggle sales calls while bouncing her on his knee. This helped so much to get a few straight hours of accounting work completed without interruption.

Balancing home life with work life was the life I knew with my first child. Each day I somehow managed to get eight hours of work done within four to six hours of time. But sometimes I'd need to finish work late into the night or on weekends. The rest of the time was for diaper changes, feedings and playtimes. It wasn't a perfect system, but we did what was needed to succeed.

When Sami went off to preschool, I missed her and looked forward to picking her up at the end of each day. Work stopped and play began until dinner, bath and bedtime. We were a happy family of three. Meanwhile, our business kept growing.

We had multiple truckloads of stone in transit all across the nation, all hours of the day. With so many trucks on the road, tracking them was a necessity to ensure on time deliveries. We worked within different states, which meant working in different time zones. It was common for the phone to begin ringing at 5 a.m. Pacific Time to accommodate customer questions back east.

As we grew, frequent travel was fundamental to ensuring success. Scott was away from home for weeks at a time. I stayed back at corporate headquarters while he traveled back and forth to our multiple locations.

We made all the tough decisions. Decisions such as hiring and firing people. Decisions on finances and expansion. Product lines, distribution center locations, accounting, technology, personnel and equipment required to grow. We set up protocols and employee manuals. Safety programs and training. It seemed whenever workload became too full, it was time to create and hire for another position in our company.

It took many years, but our hard work paid off. We had built a successful, $30 million a year natural stone business that spanned four states; we had five subsidiary companies; and we employed over 250 people nationwide. It grew beyond anything we could ever imagine. We took a step back and with grateful hearts, took a breath.

We had finally reached a place in our business where we could take time away from the office. It was uncommon for my husband and I to allow ourselves time off from work through those many years of growth. But, that same growth later produced excellent managers, supervisors and employees within the company. This allowed us more time away from the office.

And so my husband and I were finally able to do what we had always wanted, and that was to also build up our personal life. Our successful business provided an upgraded living. We acquired more land and started to build the custom home of our dreams. Sami was 6 years old then, and we were also preparing for the birth of our second daughter, Jenna. My dream of retiring as a stay-at-home Mom was about to come true. I never felt more blessed. It was all so satisfying to work hard and to reap the benefits.

Jenna was born one day after we moved into our home. Now instead of working at our business, I faced the task of caring for a new baby girl and her big sister, and running our beautiful home. This was to be my work now, and I loved it. I welcomed a whole new world of furniture choices and decorating; at the same time, I was taking care of diapers, feedings, naps and play times.

It was the first and only time of my life I have not had to balance my mommy responsibilities with managing the office. Instead, my life now centered around them: cheer practice, play dates and running endless errands. For three years, I dove hook, line and sinker into the world of mommy hood. We attended story time and activities at the local library. I involved myself in carpooling, volunteering at school, and a new puppy. The kids attended swim lessons and gymnastics lessons as I was happy to be a mommy taxi. I even taught myself how to cook!

As years passed, Sami ventured further into her long standing world of cheerleading. Jenna started preschool, attending four short hours per day. Jenna and I spent a lot of time swimming or taking walks. We found joy in collecting leaves, rocks, flowers, and anything along our path. We also kept busy doing household chores together. She found joy helping me. She helped me fold laundry, clean up and cook meals; she was my biggest little helper. Days of house work, school schedules and homework. Activities, cheer practice and evening routines. Life was busy.

The business continued to thrive and we managed our finances well. We were always careful and methodical about our budget. Years later, we came to add recreational luxuries we had only dreamt of.

Our financial position allowed us to assist my parents as well, providing a house for them to retire in. The physical health of both my parents was in decline, so being able to care for them was a welcome relief. It was something we had always wanted to do, and we felt happy to do it.

Even with increase, we were not frivolous. Budgeting was always on the forefront of our minds. Now we were on the way toward our five-year plan of having all loans paid in full, including our home. Often we took a step back and marveled at our good favor.

We were also finally able to take the kids on trips to the beach or escape to the lake at a moment's notice. Enjoying time away from work, allowing ourselves time to rejuvenate. It was necessary. Being able to create family memories together was priceless, and we appreciated every minute of it. Sometimes, my parents or other family members joined us. This created memorable moments for the kids to cherish, too. My favorite memories of the girls' childhood were being on the water. The waves of the lake guaranteed to relax them into a gentle sleep.

They grew up traveling with us on beach trips. They played in the sand and rode their battery powered mini quads around camp. We enjoyed gathering friends together to entertain either at home or away on the lake or beach. We always included our kids.

Life was as perfect as I could imagine. We had a business we were proud of. We had our precious growing family, and we were soaking in every minute of it! We were honest, hard-working, and thankful.

Little did we know this was the year we'd discover our world was about to crumble. That a huge storm was forming and headed our way.

Life is so unpredictable. So often we go through life comfortable that we'll go to work, do our job, come home and take care of the house and family. We cash our paychecks on schedule. We thrive, budget and rely on that income to establish the lifestyle we enjoy.

We thought we were set. We never considered that everything we worked so hard for could be destroyed in a blink of an eye. We thought it would be around forever. But that's not what happened to us.

We were in the eye of a perfect storm.

TWO

Facing the Unexpected

Our demise wasn't from poor management, or spending too fast, or not minding the store. Storms rarely happen because you make them happen; they are almost always out of your control.

No, ours happened in 2008—the year that will go down in history as the housing market crash. We now know it to be the perfect storm of economic collapse and banking crisis in the United States. Being in a construction or real estate business, or any business using the wrong bank, could face immediate trouble.

As with many businesses, in the building materials trade, ours had busy months and less busy months. That's known as a seasonal business. So, each year we secured a bank line of credit (LOC) to help cash flow our slower winter months. Many businesses do this to make sure they have the necessary cash flow month in and month out. Our line of credit was with, let's call them "Bank A," and renewed for over 10 years. Each year, we borrowed to get through our winter months and each year we paid off our LOC at the height of our season. We always had plenty in the busy months to off-set the off-season months. We had a great, long standing relationship with Bank A.

But then, we moved out of the eye of the storm. Overnight, the storm slammed into us.

One morning we woke up and saw the announcements on the news that Bank A was going bankrupt. Out of nowhere our bank was in trouble? Our hearts dropped! But instead of bankrupting, "Bank B" swooped in at the stroke of midnight and bought them out. What was so terrible about that? Sounded like good news to me, too, but there was one small problem. Bank B decided they would no longer continue with Bank A's business model of offering business line of credits.

Once again, a change happened overnight. The takeover of Bank A from Bank B was a big part of the 2008 banking crisis. We just happened to be in the wrong place at the right time for this storm.

The bank takeover diminished any chance for us to continue with our usual line of credit. In almost an instant, Bank B decided they wouldn't honor Bank A's line of credit business model. We were blindsided by the change in terms, but even more so by the new timeline.

Either we must pay back the line of credit amount *in full within a week* or Bank B would begin the process of extracting funds right out of our business. They would break down our company piece by piece until there was nothing left.

Nothing.

After all our decades of hard work. Late nights. Sacrifices. People we employed. Customers we supplied. Exclusive vendor relationships we built. All of it flashed before my eyes.

We did not have all the money to pay back the LOC overnight and wouldn't for a while. We were into our off season. What could we do? We scrambled. We stressed. We prayed for a miracle.

Our excellent payment history did not matter to Bank B. Nor the potential future or strength of our company, or the longevity of what we worked so hard to build. It was either pay now or watch destruction. It all seemed so unfair. How could this be happening?

We felt they were treating us harshly, and we had everything to lose, so we fought it. We had a fight on our hands and things were about to get worse before they got better. Our nights became sleepless and our days fraught with despair.

And so, our five-year, debt-free plan we had made for ourselves was cut short in year three. The storm caused us to drop everything and put all our energy into fighting.

Our fight with Bank B continued over the next five years. Through those five years, we simply watched as the rules and covenants continued to change out of our control. We were business owners trying to follow the rules, but the rules took on a life of their own, and we were at the mercy of them. We just shook our heads. We couldn't believe this was happening. We were honest, hard working business owners, and none of that seemed to matter now. The chaos had begun.

The loan covenant changes demanded approximately $1.3 million to be paid back as we headed into our winter season. Equivalent to about $250,000 a week for six to eight weeks. It wasn't long before the subsidiary companies felt the brunt of the storm. The bank would take all the income and leave the debt. It felt like a tornado coming in, picking and choosing what it wanted to take.

When you start to lose part of the business you spent so long building, you start to lose a part of yourself.

Our first wave of loss was the closure of our subsidiary companies. So, each time one of our subsidiary companies was forced to shut down, the burden fell on the parent company. The debt passed along without the revenue to support it. It was as if the storm had knocked the power out, and there was no other means of light or resources.

Despite that challenge, we were successful in downsizing our business. Through each phase, we also downsized our personal life to continue the fight for its duration. We had hopeful, prospective buyers for the business during this time as well. But unfortunately, no one wanted to move fast enough for Bank B's requirements. With the economy in such a questionable state, the clock was ticking.

To make matters worse, this obstacle put us in the position of losing both of our incomes. Sooner or later, our time and cash would run out. We weren't sure how we would live and care for our two girls.

The unexpected was about to rule our lives.

Is it possible to build new dreams after such devastation? Can you overcome the negativity and insecurities from losing everything and coming back stronger? Will your relationships withstand the devastation of hitting rock bottom and losing everything?

This was just the beginning. The storm kept coming and wouldn't stop. We had to think on our feet in preparation for the worst case scenario. We worked to sell our personal assets in haste, never looking back. We sold everything we could to downsize and put ourselves on a strict, no frills budget.

It felt like we were selling memories. Memories of kids swimming and playing on the lake. Memories of friends and family vacationing together on epic wake boarding and tubing adventures. Memories of caravan adventures with friends to the beach. Epic quad adventures in the sand dunes and camping fun in our home away from home.

It felt as though a part of us died and my heart broke as each piece left our possession. We had to ride out the storm and hope we could extend our income as long as possible during our fight. Of course, we knew it was all just stuff, but at the time it was what it represented. None of that mattered now.

It was all about survival.

We ended up having to sell my parents' house, the home we purchased for them eight years prior. My father's business closed during those years, due to his deteriorating health. We purchased a home for them near us so they could live independently. At the time of our storm, they had been in and out of the hospital multiple times. Out of options, my parents moved into an assisted living facility as a result of their failing health. How heartbreaking it was to not be able to care for them in their greatest time of need. No other family members were in a position to help out. We were out of options.

In an effort to hang onto the business as long as possible—hoping all the while that the economy would turn around, or Bank B would listen to reason, or some other miracle would happen—we decided to forgo our usual management draws from our own company. We had no incoming salary. Many business owners do the same in times of crisis, because their business is their baby. So watching it crumble piece by piece, while you can't do anything about it, is like watching your most prized possessions being carried away by a hurricane.

We hoped it would be only a few months, but it ended up being a few years. We made it work as best as we could. It was more important for us to bankroll the salaries and wages and keep our employees as long as possible. Since we were now surviving on our savings, selling our assets and cutting living expenses would extend our money. We always kept hope we could save our business and win our fight with the bank. At the same time, no one knew how long this downturn would last.

Each day I went to work with butterflies in my stomach so severe, no food would stay down. I walked around the office weak in my knees from nerves on end. I couldn't take full breaths as my chest felt weighted down. The weight of the world was on my shoulders. My mind flooded with fearful, scary thoughts of having to close our business. I didn't want to end up on the streets. I had to dig down deep to focus on each task at hand, when all I wanted to do was run away fast!

As time marched forward, to make ends meet, we had to sell our new house. It was a hard and sad decision. Our beautiful dream home went on the market, and we hoped for a quick turnover. It was our hope to preserve our remaining cash for the uncertain future and survive the next few years.

This step was especially hard for me, because of what this home represented. This was the home we thought we'd be in forever. The home we worked decades for. The home we could see our daughters married in. The home we chose every use of space throughout. The attention to detail. Each item chosen to create a warm inviting space for family and friends. The kitchen, designed for serious cooking. The wall to wall windows allowing natural light and beauty to shine throughout the home. The wrap around balcony from the master bedroom. The views from the hills that we never got enough of. This house was an extension of ourselves. All soon to be a distant memory and sure to sell so fast we'd have to move out within a month.

We were heartbroken. We were terrified.

There are plenty of ups and downs in business, and we had seen our share over the years. What we did not count on was the U.S. economic downturn to not only ruin our livelihood, but make it difficult to sell our house. The lack of buyers as the subprime mortgage market crashed.

We needed our expensive house to sell pronto in a slow market. It was the one game changer in our personal financial scenario. Otherwise, the bank would own it soon enough. All our fighting and perseverance would have been for nothing. It was crazy riding the emotional roller coaster of finances, failing parent health, and fighting for our business. Our world continued collapsing.

One thing I have learned along the way is to look for glimmers of sunshine or to be grateful for the rain or wind. Sometimes rain and wind are necessary, even though we'd rather the weather was normal again. I tried my best to be grateful as the storm marched on. We all need something to hold onto, something solid we can count on to keep us from blowing away.

I'm so thankful my relationship with my husband became stronger. Instead of falling apart while experiencing a financial crisis in our marriage, we bonded together. We were tested to the limits. We had each other to cry with, shake in fear, throw up from nerves and stay awake night after night with worry.

Many issues may arise when finances change in a marriage: arguments, anger, jealousy. The strain and pressure of dwindling finances can break down even the strongest relationships. One blames the other for the mess they're in. Or feel angry because of desperate times. They feel confined by not being able to spend like they used to, or hate the situation they're in. We relied and depended on each other through the toughest times. And for that I am grateful. Our relationship sustained me during this storm.

In October 2010, the doorbell rang. A real estate agent stood before us with exciting news. She began explaining she had an incredible offer and a large deposit in hand toward the sale of our home! Could this have been the break we were waiting for? Had we done it? Had we actually been able to sell our home in what seemed like a doomed market? It was the calm in the storm that we desperately needed.

A tiny breath of excitement filled my soul. Our newest challenge presented itself; we needed to find a different place to live, stat! This buyer wanted a 20-day escrow and was willing to pay more to have us out ASAP. Who were we to question that request at the time? We accepted the challenge, found a house through a mad search and made an offer!

I remember the next few days as if they were yesterday. It's definitely where comfortable and familiar completely fell apart. It was October 30, 2010, when we placed an offer contingent on our home finalizing. That day, we were volunteering at our daughter's school Harvest Fair. I was directing traffic at this popular event when my cell phone rang. It was my husband telling me that the offer on our home was a scam—it wasn't real. The escrow $400,000 check that had been overnighted to the real estate agent was *not real*. It was intended to trick the title company out of cash.

Here's the scam: The title company would cash the check as normal. A few days later, the scammers would call and ask for the money back (as if they changed their minds about the purchase) in hopes the check hadn't cleared the bank yet. Once the title company would tell them they already cashed the check, the scammer would request a wire replacement payment instead. Gone would be the money, as well as the scammers disappearing —leaving the title company with an insufficient funds check and a drained bank account.

Unfortunately, the title company was unable to trace or catch the scammers. But they had recognized a similar transaction from earlier months, which is why they caught this one when they did. Our title company had unfortunately already experienced one loss of this nature earlier in the year. They were able to catch wind before this check cashed and the money gone forever. When the title company called to verify funds of the check, they learned the account was a fake.

There was an emptiness in the pit of our stomachs; an emptiness that burrowed a permanent hole in us. Despair filled our hearts. All our hopes of recouping the money from our dream home were dashed in a second.

My heart sank further as the news sunk in. I tried to wrap my brain around how this had happened. Or more so, how did this storm within a storm happens *to us*? Hadn't we been through enough? Someone was playing a joke on us, right? Our one shot of something going right in a world crashing down around us had vanished. It was the beginning of a series of unfortunate events to follow.

Because when it rains, it pours.

Next, something happened that would have been enough loss on its own. Over the next year, I lost many family members who I loved dearly.

Two days after we learned of our house outcome, my mother passed away. Then my aunt, who had been diagnosed with liver cancer in July 2010—she passed the following month, November 2010. My cousin followed. Then my father passed away a few months later in April 2011. Scott's father followed on my birthday, September 9, 2011.

We were crushed.

My mother had been sick as long as I could remember. She suffered from Multiple Sclerosis and was diagnosed when I was eleven. Decades of living the disease along with her, the frustration, the fear, the anger were gone the instant she passed. While I knew she was no longer in pain, so many unexpected emotions hit me. I realized she wouldn't be around to watch my girls grow up. I realized how much I needed her advice now that I was a grown up. I missed her fiercely.

I was happy my aunt, my Mom's sister, would still be with me with the absence of my Mom. We became closer than ever. She would come visit the girls as much as she could and it was wonderful to be able to have adult conversations with her and share in the trials and tribulations of mommy adventures. Something I didn't have as my Mother's disease took over.

My aunt's liver cancer diagnosis was sudden and shocking. Her death even more so! In six short months—she was gone. Another funeral, more goodbyes. Two beautiful women I really needed were no longer there.

My father's health continued to decline once Mom and my aunt passed away. Knowing I would lose him too broke my heart. My Dad was my rock. He was always there to lend support or keep me company. I was with him the last hours of his life, holding his hand and doing my best to be his rock.

I never let him know how bad our situation was. I didn't want him to worry. I wanted to spend my time with him doing the things he enjoyed. My last words whispered to him before he passed took all the strength I had left. I told him I loved him. I thanked him for being my Daddy and told him I would always be okay, and now he could go be with Mom again. It was time to let him go. He passed a few hours later.

So much loss in a short period was devastating.

Grief is a storm all by itself. It's like a tornado that swirls around and around you, and you feel like you are going to get swept away, you want to hide.

I spent a lot of time feeling numb after the passing of my parents and other family. I cried daily for what seemed like months. I didn't have much energy or want to leave the house each morning, let alone get myself ready to face the day. All the while our fight with the bank ensued.

I was exhausted and terrified of the unknown future of our very livelihoods, and heartbroken from the losses in my family. I was numb on the inside, while appearing "normal" on the outside; depression had set in.

Anything that shut my mind down for a while was a welcome relief. I needed to get myself up and in the shower each day. It turned out to be a welcome relief for me; it gave me a bit of time to shut myself down and take a deep breath.

Nothing prepared us for the despair of losing so many family members in a short time. Or the agony of waiting for the phone to ring with an offer on our house. The clock tick-tick-ticking away as the economy continued to collapse.

We watched as businesses around us were shutting their doors, all the while afraid of the same demise. We were drowning in stress, fear, and depression. Life was full of uncertainty and impending doom. Days grew to months. Months grew to years.

It was two years before our house finally sold. The price negotiated in the end is too painful to even mention today; it was a short sale. Let's just say, the buyer got the deal of the century. In a way it ended like our business did—a victim of bad circumstances and bad luck.

It was the lowest of times. I had heard it said once, "That which does not kill you, makes you stronger," but when you are in the middle of it, you can't see how you could ever be stronger. You just feel weak. Sometimes it's hard to see through the storm that is pounding you in the face. It felt as though a dark cloud of doom surrounded us day and night, unrelenting. We had to put one foot in front of the other and keep pushing through the storm.

When would it end? How would it end?

I returned to work to help with further downsizing of our business. We had to lay off people left and right to downsize to appropriate levels. Amazing people. People who were willing to stick with us through an uncertain future. The bank continued to change our loan covenants and reduce our availability of cash. It further depleted our company's reserves.

I was sad to go back to work. I was scared for our future, confused about why this was happening to us and angry at the circumstance. I was determined to kick Bank B's butt and regain our company back. My anger and fear fueled me. It was then I started to learn just how much fight and determination I had in me.

But, it wasn't easy. Being back to work full time after a three-year hiatus, I had to brush up on new accounting software. I had to get back into the swing of management life AND managing home life again with the girls, Sami now 10 and Jenna now 4. I had to keep things as normal as possible during the switch of mommy not being around as I was before. It was frustrating. Stressful. Unpredictable. It brought up all kinds of anxious, angry, jealous, fearful feelings for a life I had to let go of. I was mentally exhausted already, and we had such a long journey to go.

Circumstances beyond our control spun us into the storm. We were among many of the unlucky businesses forced to close their doors during that time. The world had changed in a way we could never anticipate. The economy changed. The banking industry changed. As great as our company was, it wasn't cash rich enough to continue. The bank extracted our companies for five years. The fight to continue business through our upcoming winter season with Bank B was bleak.

March 2013 marked the end of 20 years in business. We closed up shop, and turned everything over as the bank's receivership took hold. We had fought a good fight for five years, watching as our cash was stripped away from our companies. Stripped during ever changing loan covenants, court fights and unethical behavior.

Unethical behavior such as the bank representative telling us "There are many businesses worthy of saving, but you're not one of them. We're going to do everything we can to bankrupt you." Who says that? We didn't know this person, nor did he know of us. There was no reasoning. There was just power play with a bank employee in charge of our destiny and a bank unwilling to compromise. Unwilling to assist us. This was one of many situations we faced during those years.

The bank had refused our submission of a sound, proven reorganization plan. They had too many new people in the mix and placed no effort to do anything other than extract companies. Over time, all the top executives we originally worked with when the storm began were either fired or quit half way through our journey in disagreement with bank policy and actions. Each time a new person came in, we had to start over explaining our situation. And each time we lost a bit more patience and became less fearful. Did they not have records and notes in our file?

Finally, we had had enough. We handed the keys over to Bank B and took the loss. Our time and cash ran out. Our world encompassed too much loss already. It was time to let go. Sometimes, you just have to let the storm take over and quit fighting it. Wait out the storm and pick up the pieces left from the destruction.

Our unwillingness to stress ourselves further into an early grave brought us clarity. The fight was no longer worth it. It was time to let it all go and move on for the betterment of our health, our kids and our quality of life.

But then came an ironic twist of events.

Bank B took possession of our company and placed it in receivership. They were adamant time and again in expressing to us how easy it would be to liquidate our assets. Yet, they approached Scott and asked him to sell the assets of our company for 10% commission per item sold. It turned out that the company they expected to use for the liquidation had no knowledge of our industry and their efforts were a bust. They were not going to get the return they expected on the abundant assets, nor be as easy as they'd expected and needed Scott's help.

In essence, they hired Scott as an independent contractor to sell off every last bit of his own business, piece by piece, as the money was turned over to the bank. It was a huge slap to the face. With no other immediate prospects for income and both our incomes lost, Scott was reluctant but agreed.

Sometimes in the middle of a storm, we have to do things we would never expect.

Throughout that next year, we were faced with untangling our life from the receivership. In doing so, Scott endured the pain of negotiating prices for each piece of equipment our company owned. Each pallet of stone remaining in our yard and quarry. And each parcel of property, dismantling 20 years of our life's work. It was the first time in all our years together I watched my husband shed a tear. This was the final process that broke him.

On one hand, with this opportunity he was providing for his family in a critical time. On the other, he was unable to just walk away and start fresh. He had to negotiate, communicate and work for the bank that put us in our unnecessary situation. Each day reliving the devastation and constant reminder of our failed life's work. I watched as his confidence shattered, his energy drained, and depression set in further.

Suffering through that was the hardest thing I witnessed. I cannot pretend to imagine what he felt through that time. I wished so many times that I could close my eyes and it would all go away.

Unfortunately, that is not how it works. Storms come in and out of our lives whether we want to or not. And so, we pressed on.

THREE

There's Always a Choice

Part of our clarity came as we made the choice to let go. Storms may come, and while we don't have control over where they land or how powerful they are, we do have power over something: ourselves. We can control how we react, where we go, what we do, and how we deal with that storm. We also have control over our attitude about that blasted storm.

I love this quote: "'Show me your worst,' the Earth said to the storm, 'and I will blossom anyway.'"

Choices make the difference between succeeding or giving up. To be able to make a decision and make another, moving forward until we come up with a resolution or solution. Back when we were in the middle of our storm, my husband and I had a choice each morning upon waking: a choice to give up or to make something positive happen that day.

Some days the choice was as simple as a smile or laughter. Others, it was a win at work, or the ability to be in the moment with the kids or as a family unit. Daytime became much easier to face, because night was when the mental chatter took over.

As the fight ensued, each night my hubby and I would hold each other and cry out of fear for losing everything. This was the only time we allowed ourselves to feel the impact of the situation. To feel and talk out loud about how we would support ourselves, feed the kids, and provide for their futures. How would we care for ourselves if we lost everything we had? We had to face all those scary possibilities.

We wept about losing the beautiful life we created. The dream life we worked hard to build and not take for granted. We felt sorry for ourselves for only a few brief moments each night. It was during those private, vulnerable times together that we found strength. To allow ourselves to really feel the impact of our situation. To grieve. It kept us moving forward. We would never mention that vulnerability to anyone. Not our kids, our family, nor our closest friends. It was ours to share during those moments.

Sleep came late into each night. Night was when the negative thoughts flooded our minds. The thoughts of failure, homelessness, collapse. Where the dark shadows of the mind wandered. Thoughts about the impact of the abundant amount of stress we were living. How it may later affect our health. I remember clearly to this day the feelings of suffocation it produced within my body.

The thoughts of not being able to win our fight and regain our company. The exhaustive thoughts of rebuilding it if we won. Would we have the strength and desire to build it again after 20 years of blood sweat and tears? The thought of what we'd do if we had to start over; what we'd do for work. Would we work for someone else after being self employed our whole lives? Were we even employable? We were both older than we were the first go around.

The thoughts of failing our little girls, being without a home or income. Thoughts of my hubby or myself passing away from stress-related health issues. Leaving our kids alone with no finances to protect them.

We cried until we were sick of it. Some thoughts were validated worries and others, negative gibberish. Gibberish brought on by the anxiety we were living. Our situation was horrible beyond belief. It depleted our confidence and took the spark out of our fire as each day passed.

It was helpful to allow ourselves time to feel our bottled up emotions. Emotions we tucked away during daylight hours. We had to put on our brave, strong, persona of leadership at work and in front of the kids. The process of airing our concerns, feeling everything and saying all those words out loud, and sharing our scary thoughts together, helped us weed through the negativity and pin point the reality of our situation. This process helped us figure out what we could do. It also allowed us the ability to change focus and make choices to rise above. Without it, we wouldn't have been able to make the choice to crawl out of it and not dwell in the pity. To recognize that as horrible as our situation was, many people are suffering daily from much worse.

Can you overcome the negativity and insecurities and rebuild yourself after losing everything? Can you come back stronger? You can if you put your mind to it! Again, it comes down to choices. Do you choose to listen and believe every negative thought that fills your mind? Or do make the effort to turn those thoughts around?

Choose to get through each day with purpose. Focus good energy on trusting things will work out. Change negative feelings to manifest the best of the situation. In my experience, having trust and faith is important through difficult times. It brings a person out better off than before.

Oftentimes, it's difficult to see how such a life dilemma can bring something good in the future.

The old adage remains true: when doors close, others open. The trick is being open to finding those doors and taking a step through! To work on becoming better with our reactions and thought processes. Have belief to pull through tough times, trust everything will work out and never, ever give up.

Once you realize you have the power to evoke your own change, you have the knowledge of knowing better. Staying in the negative is a choice, being bitter is YOUR choice. Being diligent and working through the situation is also a choice. Making choices is how fear is faced. You feel the fear and take action anyway, perpetuating forward motion. Every time you dive into your fear, you build more resilience. It's the strength required to get through that challenge and handle it.

You'll find the better the outlook gets, the better you get. Trust your confidence and know you can change your outlook - no matter what life throws at you.

Remember, the greatest part about the storms of life is that they pass. I cannot tell you how many times I told myself, "this will pass." It helped me keep things in perspective, especially when I had a bad day. But, I didn't lose hope—EVER!

We didn't always know what the next answer or plan would be, but we knew we had a choice to make one. We prayed for guidance, peace and direction often. Life became bigger than the two of us. Not only did we have to put our faith forward into the future, but also trust the direction we were heading. We gave everything to God and trusted we'd come out better on the other side.

I'd later learn this series of events was meant to shape my future into something unexpected. This is usually the case when those doors open.

It was time to take a deep breath, tie our shoes and get to work. The storm did finally wind down. The storm in all its glory came to a pitiful end. We said goodbye to our old lives, dusted ourselves off, and went in search of the sunshine again.

FOUR

Embracing the Unexpected

As stressed out as we were during and after our storm, we didn't want our kids to know the depth of what we were facing and worry about us or about money.

Our stress was not theirs, and they were far too little to fill their lives with this kind of worry. We made the decision to keep the kids' lives as normal as possible during the storm. It was important we put our best face forward each day and be as present as we could when we were together. Thank goodness for preschool and elementary school to help fill the hours in the day. It gave us a break from always being "on."

It was during this life change that we really evaluated the reality of our situation. We had been used to a certain way of living, and that was all gone. Losing the money wasn't about status—that didn't matter to us. We both came from frugal beginnings. It was about losing the security of having money stored away for the future. Having it around when we needed it. Having savings stored up gave us peace of mind. It was soon to be gone and we had to change our focus.

The first step was for us to embrace that life wasn't going to be the same anymore; in fact, it was going to be unexpected and unpredictable. Coming back from the devastation of this storm was going to take a ton of energy and hard work for many years. But until that happened, we had to make a new plan. We started to become ok with that. Heck, we had survived the storm so far, and we were still here.

Next, we had to rebuild. What does that mean? It's different for everyone, and we were definitely learning different things as we went along. Thankfully, we did have some skills that helped us. For one thing, we knew how to budget. But now it was time to take it to a whole new level.

Since the time our kids were young, we took the opportunity to teach them the value of money. We wanted them to be able to distinguish the difference between needs vs wants. They became good about figuring out that most of their requests were wants.

When our lives changed, we didn't allow items in that weren't a necessity. It pained me to pass on little trinkets at the stores as we ran errands. Birthday parties, Scholastic book sales, eating out, school or fund raising donations became luxuries we could no longer afford. I had to say "no" most all of the time.

Eating out was rare. If we did eat out as a family, it was at a local restaurant using a coupon saver "buy one get one free" meal. We shared meals with the kids and ordered no extra beverages, just water.

I cooked the majority of our meals at home, which turned out to be a great thing for us. I decided to only buy veggies, meats and healthy fats. Cooking delicious meals was essential to our budget and shopping success each week. This enabled the family to continue to eat healthy food. This cut expensive extras out of our grocery bill. We eliminated processed foods and nourished our bodies during stressful times.

Out of necessity, I used everything in the pantry and refrigerator before heading to the store again. We ate soups, stews, leftovers and lots of egg scrambles. We got creative. This finished off remaining ingredients each week. Cooking was one of our main forms of inexpensive family entertainment.

We stopped paying for morning mochas at the local coffee drive-thru. We became familiar with the clothing in our closets. Clothes were worn until they were completely worn out or the kids grew out of them. We cut the cable bill, water and electric use, phone bills, television—anything that helped reduce our monthly living expenses.

I clipped weekly coupons and searched thrift stores. I found deals on clothes and toys at yard sales when necessary, and friends provided hand me downs for the kids. Anything necessary to continue to live our "normal lives." I shopped only at the retail stores where I could use my cash rewards and coupon savings. We did everything we could to save money and fundraise for our kids' activities to keep them busy.

I remember the fall of 2013 like it was yesterday. I was so afraid of Christmas coming and not having the money to pay for gifts. I wasn't ready for the magic of Santa Claus to be over for our girls. I was desperate, so three months prior, I began selling items on an online yard sale site. I hoped to collect enough money to make a small Christmas happen. It took a great deal of hustle, but I did it! I even had enough money left over to buy a small tree from the Boy Scouts that year. Christmas, accomplished! It felt good to have those little successes.

Staying healthy was a big priority for me. I considered my health a non-negotiable "need." If you want something bad enough, you'll find a way to make it happen. So I negotiated my gym membership rates. This wasn't something I was willing to give up, so I cut back on other things to make those payments happen.

We were fortunate to trade in our gas guzzling SUV. Especially because this was a time when gas prices were soaring over $5 a gallon in California. We decided on a Volkswagen Passat for its amazing gas mileage and leg room for the kids. We actually took the hit out of our savings for this one to pay for the car in full. This decision alone saved us over $1,000 per month on fuel and car payments.

We held frequent family and friend game nights to be social. We asked them to bring a dish to have a pot luck style dinner. This inexpensive option helped feed everyone and provided for hours of free entertainment.

I became an expert at not spending on extras and finding free and low cost activities to do with the kids. We walked, danced to music, played outside, and collected colorful fall leaves. We drew pictures and colored with crayons and colored pencils from the Dollar Store. We painted with watercolors and played flashlight tag at nighttime. Of course there was always cooking together, doing chores and reading stories to keep us busy.

When all was said and done, we were able to pay off all personal outstanding loans. We moved into a beautiful rental, drove a debt-free car and kept the kids entertained. We had no outstanding debt and a little savings to help us for a short while. We budgeted life, surviving on needs not wants. We were lucky and did just fine.

The sunshine was out and growing stronger.

Something amazing happens when you hit bottom and start rebuilding—you get to know what you are made of. You also realize that you can survive on very little material possessions. You become resourceful and less wasteful, taking nothing for granted. We were so lucky to have each other. We had strengthened relationships by being in the present moment and being awake to everything around us. Kids who were happy and thriving without knowing the better of what we were going through.

Even with all the loss around us, we remained blessed. Blessed because we had the choices available to us each day. To either make the necessary changes or face defeat. The ability to make those changes always kept us in perspective that things could ALWAYS be worse.

FIVE

The Power of Relationships During Storms

My husband, Scott, my best friend, was there through good times and bad—never leaving my side, never looking back, never faltering. Yet all the while, he had his own fears and doubts. That strength and vulnerability in our relationship was the greatest of the many gifts the storm brought us. Of course, it was difficult to see all the gifts delivered during the storm, but as time passed and the skies cleared, they became clear. I believe something wonderful comes out of the darkness if you choose to allow it. That belief is a part of my "cup is half full" outlook on life.

We confided in each other to determine the next plan of action as we faced the next decision that needed to be made. Our two other business partners wanted no part in the hard, tough times; we bore the fight alone. It's funny what you learn about people during such an experience. When we were on top, they wanted all the glory, but when it all hit the fan, no one was there. I'm sure they faced their fear in their own ways, but for us, it was a tiring, draining, lonely time. We had to have faith and let go: letting the small things go and giving the bigger problems to God because they were beyond our control. It was the first time for both of us to really test our faith.

We gave up our pride and egos when we hit rock bottom. We prayed together while snuggling in each other's arms each night before we went to sleep. Falling asleep in my hubby's arms was the safest place I knew. It was a place of reassurance, a place where I knew he'd always make sure we were alright; he was my rock, my strength, my everything. I'd later learn though, that wasn't enough. I'd also have to learn to be my own source of strength.

Our daughters thrived those years in spite of our stress, so our attempts to keep their lives "normal" was a good decision. They maintained excellent grades at school and were happy kids. We spent time being in the moment and working on what matters most in life—our relationships.

Our family unit grew tighter and together, and after so many years worrying, strategizing, planning and surviving, we were free to move on. We were fortunate, we were blessed and we appreciated each day; those gifts were priceless.

Will your relationships withstand the devastation of hitting rock bottom and losing everything? Some will and some won't. We had close friends who became acquaintances. I believe it was from fear or discomfort of having to watch us go through our business closing and our finances dwindling. Others are only meant to be in our life for a short time.

People can only give what they can of themselves, what they are comfortable with. Sadly, not everyone is prepared to go through the tough times with you. So many people in our lives disappeared once our financial status changed, the house was sold and the pool was no longer available. Other people drifted out of our lives as quickly as they arrived.

Friends I counted on to be there in my darkest times ran away as fast as they could. Unfortunately, they also chose to take the friendships of our kids with them. What a slap in the face! To this day, I don't understand the reasons for that sudden change; I was only left to speculate. In my attempt to share my deepest feelings with my closest friends, I found myself an outcast.

I'm sure the reasoning made sense for them at that time, but to walk out on a close friendship without explanation or closure feels very much like a breakup, and the abandonment hurts just the same. It left me with the task of explaining to my young daughters why their friends didn't want to play with them anymore. Not only was that unfair, but even more painful as I looked into their young, confused, hurt eyes. Fortunately, I've learned to let that go, too.

The sting from the quintessential slap across the face and the loneliness from not putting faith into new friendships lasted for many years. Family tried to be supportive, but they didn't know how. They were numb from the abundance of loss experienced from deaths in the family.

I spent years without a close girlfriend to confide in. In fact, I wasn't sure friendships like that were possible for me anymore. My mother and aunt were gone. Also, being a boss didn't leave much room for friendship when the majority of my time was spent at work with employees.

I walked around my children's school like a zombie and was unwilling to make new mommy friends. If I'm being completely honest, it was partly my fault. I stopped wanting to be social for fear of having to make small talk with these questions: "What do you do for work?" or "What have you been up to lately?" It was a conversation played out way too often and my desire to discuss our situation diminished each time I had to talk about it.

I arranged some play dates at the park for our kids with other friends because it was neutral ground. I could endlessly spin conversation and focus back to the kids: how they were growing so fast, how much they loved to swing, etc. Young kids always have the knack of interrupting grownups, so no one had time to make chit chat of work, life or long conversations.

We couldn't tell anyone what was happening to us. What could we say? "We're losing our business . . ." "We've had to sell everything in hopes to survive . . ." Neither of those were appealing conversation starters.

As I said, though, as one door closes, another one opens. Over time, we slowly began to entrust new friendships. I've since added fantastic core friendships back into my life. I don't believe we were put on this earth to go through life alone. My mistake in thinking we were not to share our dark secrets only hurt me in the end. I was just sharing with the wrong people. I now keep only a small, close group of people dear to my heart these days. Quality vs quantity, if you will.

We surrounded ourselves with people who would build us up, encourage and inspire our lives, and not bring us down with negativity. I think there's treasure in experiencing life by confiding in others, sharing memories, trusting relationships and being there for each other through good times and bad. Growth happens, relationships strengthen and most importantly, we don't feel alone in this great big world.

If we allow it, we begin to find others with like-mindedness. Those who share similar values, lifestyles and perspectives on life. It's up to us to find these people and let the toxic relationships go. Even family members can add to the toxicity levels if we're not careful. We need to fill our lives with positive energy and people who make us better each day. People you can't wait to spend time with, who improve the quality of your life by being in their presence. To be able to sit quietly together and be at peace, or to be silly and crazy and fill the days with laughter, smiles and memories.

I'm ever so grateful for the friendships I have in my life, and I'm forever changed by the impact these friendships and my experiences have had on me. I always figured close friendships were reserved for childhood, not in adult life. I'm so lucky to know that statement is not true!

Far too often, people can be insincere, selfish, self serving or self absorbed. I'm a giving person: giving of my heart, myself, my time, my soul. But being a giving person comes with a price. If I choose friendships poorly, those qualities are never returned. I must share those qualities with people who know me as well as I know myself and love every part of me. That is something I cherish and don't take for granted! Each friend inspires, encourages or challenges me in some way. I choose to have it this way. I won't stand for less; I've learned too much.

Storms test our limits and provide strength, if we allow it. There's something to be said for knowing we aren't alone in our fight, that others have been there before, too. You don't get to know that about someone without sharing. Sometimes our deepest strength within comes from knowing someone else has our back. Life support when we're not exactly sure how we'll make it through.

Having strong relationships in life provide an arsenal of support for times we are at our weakest. We can't possibly be the only pillar of strength for ourselves in this world.

SIX

Work in Progress

Although we did everything we could to combat stress, we did not come through unscathed. The timing, however, was what surprised me.

In the modern era, we now recognize that stress is the leading cause of many health issues. Stress greets you at work, in relationships, with finances, excessive exercise, or loss. We push through our days and continue to mitigate the same behaviors. We don't stop to consider how our stress can apply to us and lead to further health conditions. We just keep pushing the limits.

I'm no exception. I was well aware of the toll the daily stress took upon my health, but I had no idea the true impact that would show up later, nor how to stop it.

Once our lives began to settle back to a more peaceful time, health changes began to appear. At the time, I didn't realize they were a result of so many years of stress. So, I ignored them. At the young age of 42, I began noticing changes in my body that I never experienced before. Hard to lose inches, hot flashes, night sweats and inability to focus. Doctors would say this was due to my body beginning to age. That I was beginning to transition into a peri-menopausal state at an early age. Wait, what? "That doesn't happen until much later in life," I thought. "You must be crazy!"

I ignored the broken, lack of sleep that was normal for me. I was strong, able to lift heavy weights. I had energy to sustain hard workouts many days per week. Was it possible I wasn't in the best shape of my life?

I looked strong from the outside, but inside, something different was happening. Looking back now, I just wasn't paying attention. I always mustered up the energy to perform during my 4 p.m. workouts. But, I paid no mind to the exhaustion afterward or more so, how tired I felt beforehand. The afternoon lows I experienced each day must have been from lack of sleep, so I brushed that under the rug. My thought process became cloudy and foggy during the day. Nothing a quick cup of coffee couldn't fix. But quick fixes just mask the problem.

My body temperatures began to take a noticeable change. I'd sometimes break out in a sweat for no reason whatsoever. My anxious energy and mood changes throughout the day followed with lethargic energy. It would hit me mid-afternoon; I would crash with a sudden lack of energy in my body, but I would push through anyway.

My keen ability to stay focused, commit to a goal and never give up didn't work so well when it came to my health. I was an expert at "sucking it up." I kept going without thinking twice that something else may have been going on. I had a strange misconception that I was healthy, thus invincible.

I ignored it all for two years before I actually checked out my symptoms further. Honestly, it was because those pesky hot flashes became bigger and more of a nuisance. Otherwise, I wouldn't have bothered. I paid no attention to the exhaustion I was also experiencing in the afternoon, that it could be a sign to be concerned about, I just kept ignoring it.

Unfortunately, my body had other ideas. Do you know the human body is miraculous? It will fight and do whatever necessary to keep running at optimal level, even if it's not treated that way. It will send warning messages. In my case, warnings such as: low energy, lethargy, foggy brain, hot flashes, hair loss, stubborn body fat, disrupted sleep, mood swings, changes in my monthly cycle, aches and pains, and frequent injury.

Our body sends us messages. Signals start slowly, but because we aren't paying attention, they grow. The body will continue to send messages even if you aren't listening or paying attention to them. Then one day, it forces you to by shutting down!

Thoughts became difficult to remember, even the simple things. All of a sudden, I felt I was losing more than my car keys—I felt I was losing my mind. Thought processes and focus at work became more difficult (not convenient when your work involves numbers). The day after workouts, inflammation took hold and muscles and joints ached so much it was hard to move. Workout recovery took longer and longer. I just didn't recover as I used to.

I was desperate to sleep each night. I felt dog tired and smashed by the end of day. My mind raced as I lay down to sleep. I was wired and tired and woke often throughout the night. Add in those pesky night sweats night after night, and disrupted sleep took over my life. All signs pointed to the fact that something wasn't right in my body, and it was time to get help. I was exhausted all the time; some days I didn't want to get out of bed.

When the results of my blood test came in, they confirmed I had low levels of estrogen and progesterone, or early stages of peri-menopause. My doctor recommended Hormone Replacement Therapy (HRT) right away. So, in the months to follow, shocked as I was, I did what many women do and got started on HRT. Unaware I had other options or further testing available, I moved forward in the hope to feel better. I never once considered I may have had other underlying issues associated with my symptoms. I just took everything at face value. I never paralleled the reason why this was happening to me. Until HRT didn't work.

Conventional medicine didn't test deeper than standard blood work orders. This can oftentimes result in "normal" readings, leaving other issues undiagnosed. My test results came back within "normal" range, but I felt nothing close to normal! I had no data to support how I was feeling. In fact, adding an HRT protocol to my body at that time had an adverse reaction. It spun my hormonal systems into a frenzy. In layman's terms, I gained 15 pounds in 10 weeks and was on an emotional rollercoaster.

My cortisol levels were through the roof and showed up by way of the unwanted midsection and lower body fat gain. Results I experienced were similar to results I'd might have had after eating candy bars all those months. However, I had followed a strict diet of healthy fats, proteins, veggies, and exercised regularly. Regardless, I could not budge the gain. This was my body's way of telling me there was something else happening here. My hormone imbalances never leveled.

I was on a continuous, downward spiral of added inches and feeling crazy and unhealthy. I had to find a solution fast.

So I switched gears. I began asking better questions and took my health into my own hands. I wanted to learn more. The solutions I received were not good enough. I deserved more. I deserved to better understand what was happening to me so I could make the right decisions for myself and regain my health.

Through a Functional Medicine approach, my naturopathic doctor, and I took a closer look at what might be happening in my body and WHY. Why this was happening to me? The WHY was important so we could determine the best treatment moving forward. I was surprised this hadn't been asked of me before. So we dove into my past history. My stressful life events stood out like a sore thumb. Any one of those events could've been enough to cause a shift, but all of them together over a five-year period began to reveal a road map to the changes I experienced in my body.

My blood work and saliva tests revealed a myriad of other issues. Adrenal fatigue, a sluggish thyroid, insulin resistance and blood sugar swings to name a few. I had depleted magnesium and vitamin D levels, pre-diabetic A1C levels and digestion issues. All these systems overtaxed my hormones once I added the HRT.

I had no idea all of this was underlying at that time. There was more going on than just peri-menopause. I still hadn't connected the relationship between years of stress and my body jumpstarting into peri-menopause. But, it was the stress from years prior rearing its ugly head. It had taken its toll on my body. Weakened adrenals were working overtime to balance hormone imbalances in my body and began crashing.

We are meant to cross paths with certain people throughout our lifetime. I believe this is no accident. I happened to have a friend of mine knowledgeable in adrenal fatigue who referred me to her naturopathic physician. How fortunate I was to be able to find someone who could help me identify all those other issues. Someone who would help me understand what was happening to me. Provide testing, supplemental support and help get my body back on its healing path. The help I sought through a Functional Medicine approach allowed me to heal my body in a natural way. At least until we could get my body stabilized and establish my baseline.

This approach may not be for everyone. Just as many women experience great success with HRT, some do not at first. It wasn't what worked for me at that point in my life; in fact, it's taken almost three years to correct the damage. We detoxed my body of the HRT hormones to find my natural hormonal baseline levels. Then we'd build and repair from there, strengthening adrenal health and thyroid function.

Some days it was difficult to maintain perspective that I wasn't broken or old. I felt old and exhausted from having to deal with all this. My brain hurt from having to learn all about new changes I'd be making as well as understand the impact to my health. Perhaps I would need more hormone support in the future, but at least we had a starting point and a chance to strengthen my system before attempting it again. There was much work to do to bring balance back to my systems.

Now my body had my full attention. I was ready to address the underlying issues. I had to change the way I slept, what I ate, how and when I worked out and managed my stress to get better! I had to accept my body throughout all its changes and learn to look beyond my outer appearance.

This was the hardest time for me because I didn't want the weight gain in the first place. My body was out of my control. I had a lot of anger and frustration to let go of to get to a new level of acceptance.

My next life lesson was staring me in the face.

As long as I could recall, I maintained a healthy weight for my frame. I reaped the benefits from years of consistent food choices and exercise. I'm not someone who ever gained weight or fluctuated. The only exception was during my two pregnancies. Each time, I was able to drop that weight off within six months to a year. I was proud of all the work I'd done lifting weights and eating healthy.

But now, I had to learn to appreciate my body in its new frame and stop fighting it for my body to begin to heal. Gaining that weight, as superficial as it sounds, almost broke me. I felt so outside myself. I was uncomfortable and didn't recognize my reflection in the mirror.

My clothes no longer fit well and everything seemed to be a constant reminder of my health. I wondered if I could get past all the negative feelings within myself. To be able to value myself beyond body image and heal with the time and patience as my body was requiring. To not be in control for once and let go. It was a gut check to place my ego aside and allow my body to run its course.

How could I be so strong dealing with our life storm and so weak when it came to this personal trigger? I'm a mommy of two gorgeous girls for whom I need to be confident and strong. Feeling this way did not help me to lead by example. It did help to recognize their love for me as unconditional. It never mattered to them what my outer shell looked like. It also helped having a husband who constantly told me how beautiful I was, despite how I felt about the changes. They could all see things in me I couldn't. It was time to believe this for myself.

I had some work to do on myself. Letting go and acceptance became a recurring theme for me. Acceptance for where I was at the time was the piece of the puzzle that brought me clarity. It started me along my path of soul seeking. Seeing so much more of who I am and appreciating what my body was capable of doing or not doing in the moment. Looking beyond to see the bigger picture, if you will; knowing I wasn't broken, but a work in progress.

I won't stop learning and searching for more information for solutions to make me feel my best. I won't lose hope that I can balance out my hormones, think clearly and continue to change my body composition back to where I feel my best.

It just means that my body has worked hard to protect me from something unbeknownst to my future health. The weight was part of my process. I learned I needed to slow life down and do a better job of taking care of me: especially during times of stress. It was time to do better at keeping my cortisol levels down. Adjusting my workouts and exercise to improve the condition of my adrenals, not drain them. Time to put as much care into myself as I do everyone else in my life. Do I give up and throw in the towel because everything is harder now? No!

I stay the course. I remain diligent in the formula needed until my body reconnects to the balance it desires. The past two years, I've dropped half the inches I gained off my body by staying the course. The reward is progress toward my goal. It may be slow progress, but it's progress nonetheless!

When storms come, we may come to realize that things can never be as they were before. And that's ok. It's about progress, not being who we used to be. Learning to live life after the devastation and accepting change along the way.

I've learned that there's something to take away from the years of living a stress-filled life. It comes with a price and will rear its head sooner or later. For whatever reason, this is where I'm meant to be right now. Whether I want to be here or not is not part of the equation.

The take-away: If I knew tomorrow that going back to the body I used to have was no longer possible, I'd have to be happy now. I'd need to adapt and move on. So, I've chosen the attitude to rock what I've got and let the rest go. I've practiced eluding confidence in myself no matter what my outer shell looks like or how I feel in my skin. I practiced not accepting the negative thoughts that wanted so desperately to take over my mind. It makes such a difference in other aspects of my life as well. On my daily outlook on life.

Confidence is power. Confidence is strength.

What's inside me is so strong and powerful. I've embraced *me*! I've learned my inner strength and beauty is a much more powerful gift than I've ever known before. It's this energy, this knowledge I desire to share with my daughters and with the world. The gift I want others to realize within themselves, the same gift I want you reach for deep inside yourself. It's a choice.

If I hadn't gone through everything I did, I would not have found this clarity and appreciation. I wouldn't have made the necessary changes to be kinder to myself and keep my stress levels down. I wouldn't even know what that looks like, I'd just have continued to push hard until I dropped.

Does that mean every day is a good day? Heck no! I have bad days just like everyone. Life is messy, but I make choices to get myself out of my funk and move forward. Stress has taken its toll on my systems. It sends me a constant reminder that taking care of myself is now a priority, every day. Some days there are limits to how hard I can push. If I overdo it, my adrenals send me signals. I've become better at listening to what my body needs. There are daily limits to the foods I can eat or drink to keep blood sugar balanced. I must focus on getting enough sleep and being consistent in my food choices and taking my supplements.

Reminders that need continuous checking in with my body. Listening to what it wants. I need to be aware of my blood sugar swings, my amount of sleep, my adrenal health, my nutrition. Just the right amount of exercise, without pushing my body too much, but enough to be effective. Otherwise, I'm too tired and exhausted to be good to anyone.

My biggest take away from surviving our crazy stress storm? Never going through life without powerful tools to manage stressful events again. I was lucky. I had the instincts to pull myself through and come out stronger on the other side. I'm grateful I never gave up or gave into the pity, sorrow or fear. Having tools that work to reduce the impact of stress on the body help make me the best version of myself every day.

I look back with such gratitude for everything we experienced. I gained strength I never knew possible. I learned more about myself and what I'm capable of with appreciation I've ever known before. And I learned effective tools for coping and surviving through any storm.

Whether you believe this gift was from the universe or from God, again, it's no accident that I am here. Here, writing this book and sharing my story with you. Today, it's nice to breathe and just focus on the future one day at a time. Focus on the positive energy in my life, let creativity flow and develop into possibilities of a new future.

We are all a work in progress; so for me, my journey of learning continues into the future. That's the point in life, isn't it . . . to keep learning and bettering ourselves?! This gift has given me the strength to mold my life toward helping others achieve their greatness, too.

SEVEN

The Power to Change

I'm a "glass is half full" kind of person. I always believe something good will come from any situation. The challenge presented was something we were meant to experience to become who we are today. If you would have told me that we'd experience our series of events when I turned 40, I wouldn't have believed it. Too much at one time happening, like a movie, because you just can't make that stuff up! But it happens to all of us in one form or another at some point in our lives.

I didn't know then that we would travel to hell and back by the time we were through. Trust me, if we'd known of a way to prepare for such catastrophe, we'd have done it. But that's not how life plays out sometimes. Sometimes we must accept and learn from doing. Learn from the experience while living and feeling every step.

Is it possible to build new dreams after such devastation? Of course! Once we made the decision to let our company go and stop fighting with the bank, we set off into the world unknown. We were tapped out from the emotional loss of so many family members. The continuous battle to save our company drained all our reserves. We had to have faith even when we couldn't see the outcome.

In the end, stress was not worth losing our own health. We accepted the reality of where life was now, stopped analyzing the "why" of our situation and just let go. This WAS our life now. It was up to us to live it, change it, better it. We were in acceptance for what was.

We recognized the value of being self employed. We put our minds together and strategized a concept for a new business. We needed a backup plan ready in the wings. It would be a way for us to make income while we figured out how the rest of our life would look.

We crafted our "Plan B" and took action on forming a new company. It was a takeoff of what we knew, in a market we were familiar with. So we solved the question, "What would we do for income?" long term. The best part was, we were available to the kids before and after school. We once again had the freedom of managing our own work schedules.

It was a breath of fresh air to be onto a new chapter of our lives. By April 2013, we had moved into a rental house. We started a new business and began to see possibilities and opportunities ahead. I also started a side consulting business six months later to bridge our income gap.

At first, the consulting gig was meant to be temporary, but quickly found its niche among a downed economy, helping businesses downsize or adjust to the changes they were experiencing internally. Just like that, we had duel businesses up and running. By simply taking a leaf of faith and jumping upon opportunities as they presented themselves. This is when our rebuilding phase really started to take off.

Why then, did I have a nagging feeling that this was my chance to break free from everything I'd known before? To make a bigger change in my career and do or be whatever I wanted? To create a life that could be different from what I've always known? Was I allowed such liberty in my life? Was the collapse of our business punishment for mistakes I made in my past or a sign for better things to come?

Defeat is a funny thing. It breaks you down, piece by piece until you feel you have nothing left. Your confidence fights to stay alive and a daily battle of negativity ensues in your mind. It's a lonely, personal process. Definitely not something you want to share with others, or at least I didn't at that time. I wanted to focus on gratefulness and look for the good in life. Through that process, I realized it was never too late to be whoever I dreamed of being or do whatever I put my mind to. Even if that meant heading into a completely different field of business.

I love transformation stories. Transformations (makeovers) of any kind: beauty, construction, history, stories, mindset, life. I love to see something aged or worn revived with new life. The possibility of transforming something new again and marveling in its beauty once finished. It brings me joy.

So it came as no surprise that I began taking all this experience to a new level. I put the woes of the past behind me to work on a transformation of my own. It was time to work on me. Who am I? Who could I be now that I could become anything, anyone? What were my areas of interest? What drives me? What were my dreams and did I have the courage to seek them out?

We're all given one life to live. We choose how we spend our time living. We choose who we surround ourselves with and who we want to be. We get to make choices daily, weekly, monthly, yearly. We choose what we eat. How much we eat. How long we sleep. If we exercise, smile, laugh. If we choose to improve our situation. To stay positive in a negative world.

We have the choice of possibilities and opportunities around us. To trust our decisions and not second guess ourselves. To be the best versions of ourselves possible and continue to educate our minds. To create our destiny and fulfill our dreams.

Find a way. Find your answers. Do the work and get to know yourself. It's never too late to begin again, learn something new or work toward a goal. Live the life you want to live and make it a reality, even if it places you outside your comfort zone.

Of course, if this was easy, everyone would do it. Making this choice is hard. You have to decide. Make a decision to create change and then take one action step at a time toward your goal. Have courage and don't be afraid to learn new things. My answer to questions like "What do I want to be?" wasn't easy when I first asked it of myself. I drew a blank in my mind —I didn't know! I'd been set in my routine of life for years: building a business and caring for the family. I knew no other way.

I did learn, though, that as much as I appreciated all my years in finance and accounting, I didn't want to spend the rest of my life doing that now. The storm changed that part of life for me too much. It no longer brought me the joy it once did. It was time to move on. In that way, storms can actually be a good thing. They can wake us up and change us.

I had no clue what I'd do when I wasn't managing the finances or taking care of the family. Taking care of the house or running endless errands. It was all I knew the past 20 years. What would I do with my life if the "have tos" were actually gone and I could focus on becoming anything I wanted?

Could you answer that question? If your whole life was flipped upside down and you suddenly could rebuild it anyway you wanted, what would you do? What would you want?

I was excited to figure out the answers to those burning questions, but fear and doubt crept in to test my courage. Was I too old? Had my time passed by? Was I qualified enough? Did I have time? Would I make enough money? Wasn't it safer to just stay comfortable doing what I know?

That's what the self doubt in my mind was telling me. But once you find the strength to fight back and struggle through a storm, you are forever changed. Courage you didn't know you had pushes you forward. You begin to ignore that self doubt, acknowledge it perhaps, but move forward anyway. You believe there's more than one way to solve a problem, and every problem has a solution. Just look for the best possibility at that time and follow through. Make one decision and then make another, without fear or judgment.

You learn that the things you feared work themselves out by working through the situation. The things you worried most about never played out the way you thought they would. In the end, they were more manageable than anticipated. Step by step, decision by decision, you get through it. You build confidence in your decisions. You make a decision, then another, or change your mind and choose again. A little success and those decisions drive you to try again and again. You soon realize your mindset is the inner strength and power YOU already have within to heal!

You begin to leave the negative mind behind and search for the positive and possible. The fog lifts and your mind clears from the haze. You begin to believe in yourself. Hold your head high and recognize your skills and talents. Sometimes even new talents emerge as you discover from within. Don't be afraid to reinvent yourself with those new talents or keep reinventing yourself and time passes.

Through surviving our storm, I learned I'm a leader. I enjoy taking control of my destiny and I have the ability to encourage others. I'm self-motivated and meet goals I set for myself. I want to develop on these things in my life.

I found an answer to the burning question, "What would you be if you could be anything?" It rang in my ears. Perhaps it had been there all along, and I just wasn't listening? But I heard it, loud and clear, and my transformation began.

I wanted to write. To share my passions. It's an outlet to inspire others to identify their inner strengths and come out amazing on the other side. This led to the challenge of writing a book and voila!

I have also always had an interest in fitness and nutrition. I began to see myself becoming a strength and conditioning coach, even if only a few hours a week. So, I finally stopped thinking about it and took action. I became a coach, helping others achieve their wellness goals and encouraging them to live their most empowering life possible.

We lived through rock bottom and had nothing else to lose in our adventure. Something happens to a person with nothing to lose. Fear is no longer in the equation, and that is when strength takes over. What a great gift that is and how valuable to use this lesson throughout all areas of life! For us, decisions became easier to make, and we no longer allowed ourselves to be pushed around. We were in control of our destiny and used any doubt as fuel for success.

I believe in myself and my abilities and will not let fear win. I desire to help others, give back the knowledge I've been fortunate to learn and share my voice. I cannot encourage you enough to make the time to learn about yourself and see where that journey takes you. Make a transformation of your own; never stop learning and searching.

I value myself more these days than I ever have before in my life. I've learned I am worthy, loving, strong, intelligent, determined, focused and resourceful. I'm also protective, inspiring, hopeful, encouraging and giving. Creative, talented, funny, athletic, happy and empowering. That's a lot of adjectives, but it has taken me 48 years to believe in them.

I wouldn't have figured it out without every good and bad experience life brought me. If I never learned to love myself first, it wouldn't be possible to help others today. That's the greatest transformation of all!

I am forever changed and will not allow myself to look back.

EIGHT

Lessons Learned

Life happens. When the perfect storm shows, it's unexpected and unfortunate in circumstance.

Never in all the years of building our business did I ever think of a time when it wouldn't be there. I never thought this could happen to us. It was like this child we nurtured together, molded, shaped, structured. Always searching for ways to make our company better. To make us better as managers and the leaders of the company. We dreamed of providing a strong, happy workplace for our employees. For a moment in time, we had that and it all came to an end. But again, life happens.

Life will always offer a storm of some kind. When that storm hits, it will usually be something that flips your world upside down. Something personal to take away from it.

It happens to everyone at one point or another. It comes disguised as death of a loved one, divorce, loss of a job or a business. Perhaps a devastation from Mother Nature, a fire, or substance abuse. Deteriorating health, relationships, finances, career change, etc.—you get the point. Something that causes you to just take cover, bear down and ride through until the storm passes and the skies clear. It will require using mental, physical and emotional tools for survival.

Today, long after the storm, we'd like to think the past is behind us. But, all too often we discover some things just take more time. Someone always remembers what you used to have and loves to bring up the past. Oftentimes spoken without thought that it could be a painful memory. It brings our past shortcomings to our attention, and it feels like we'll never begin again. Our scary, uncomfortable story people would rather judge first rather than show compassion or understanding. It's far too easy to stir the pot and make assumptions about someone's loss rather than ask for the hard details.

Many real estate agents in town know the story of our beautiful dream house on the hill. Searching for a new home of our own nowadays becomes an interesting process when those dots are connected. But, we've learned it doesn't define who we are. For us, there's more to life than money. I tried to not feel anything about that beautiful home except relief that we got out from underneath it. Even better, we got out of it without drowning. We left and never looked back.

Recently, my youngest daughter wanted to take a ride with her friends to go drive by the "big" house. So I obliged her. She couldn't quite remember it well because she was so little when we left. She'd been talking to her friends about it since they lived in a nearby neighborhood. It wasn't until the moment of driving past our old home that I realized what we'd built together.

The sting of that life experience still hurts and is real no matter how much I attempt to deny it. The blood, sweat and tears that went into every detail. The seven years of watching our family grow there. The decades of hard work and sacrifice it took to get there. The business we built together that provided such an opportunity. Flashbacks of designing a home our daughters would marry in. All gone.

If you have been through something, and if you think you have moved past it, there will be times that it will haunt you. Loss is so hard. We had lost so much in such a short time. I remember looking at our old house that day, mourning a past life. Everything is so different now. Not good or bad, just different.

Yet, a house is just a thing. The new owners have since changed the color of the garage doors. They've personalized it by placing large statues in the yard. They've made changes to the landscape. It no longer looked to me like the same bright, shiny beacon it once was; it wasn't "us" anymore. The lesson here was that our "home" wasn't really the place we lived in. It was the people and memories we filled in it. That's what made it our home. Our home will always be wherever *we* are, together. Small or big, it doesn't matter. Time heals, people grow, life changes.

The storm may beat us down, but we lived through it. Wiser. Stronger.

Nowadays, we focus on securing our future. We are past the mid marker of life now. We've one shot left to plan for our senior years and save up the money needed for retirement. We've watched the clock tick as our kids have grown. We've only a small window left for family vacations and traveling together. That's where we place our time and energy these days.

Nine years have passed in a flash, and those little girls of ours? One has graduated high school and is in college and the other, six grade—middle school. It's scary how fast time goes by. Seems like yesterday they were just 9 and 3 years old. We had been through so much those years and that time with our kids flew by faster than ever. In a blink of an eye, toddler-hood turned into teenage years. Our two girls are strong, young women now and their childhood is almost over. We remind ourselves to be present each day and breathe in every moment before it's gone. That gift will remain with us for the rest of our lives. We are all onto new, changing chapters.

All of a sudden we have extra cars, insurance and fuel to budget for or pay for outright. Tires, college and wisdom teeth extraction to pay for. The list continues on as they grow, but we continue to budget and save. Lessons we learned through our storm still serve us well today.

We impress upon our children to save the money they earn. We encourage them, when they do spend it, to be sure it's something they want. We want them to work toward earning it.

We are big on having them buy their own electronics: iPod, phone, etc. We've adopted the "if you want it, earn it" mental-ity. When they use their own money, they learn to work toward a goal. Work and save toward something they desire so they learn the value of a dollar. They have more skin in the game when it comes to taking care of their treasures. Lessons that will serve them their whole lives.

Our oldest is learning to apply these skills as she enters the working world. She's learning to balance life, school and work. Learning to make and reach for her own dreams all the while learning what a true cost of living is. She's facing a new reality of her own, but I'm confident she has the tools to get her through. That's a great natural transformation story of its own!

Our experience has definitely affected our decisions on future spending as well. Big items like a house, car, etc., when we do plan to buy, although it may take much longer to get there, we'll pay for them outright. It's nice to have things paid in full! No bank or lender can ever take them away.

Memories have become more important than things. Preparing for our later years means we will not have to suffer the end of life both my parents suffered. They lost everything they built at an age they couldn't rebuild. They had no security for their future, no plan. Their children were left with the task of handling all of their end of life details.

We had to be conservators for both my parents. Watching their health decline while they wasted away in a nursing home made me angry. Angry that they didn't make provisions for themselves when they could. After they both passed, I realized we needed to do everything we could to prepare for our own futures. We needed specific instructions to not burden our children with unplanned health directives. We needed to ensure we have proper health care coverage. We needed a will.

In the meantime, we aimed to keep our minds and bodies as active and healthy as possible for the betterment of our future. It's a surreal experience having to make those decisions from the perspective that we are no longer alive or capable of making them for ourselves. It makes me sad to think of life without my children, let alone their lives without us. But I couldn't feel stronger that it's a necessity and one of the greatest gifts we can give them as parents. I don't ever wish upon them the experience I went through having to be responsible to make such heavy decisions for my parents.

Never once feeling old enough or even qualified enough to do so. The pain involved in every minute of that experience was horrendous.

Strengthen your relationships with friends and family. Those relationships are the greatest gifts we have and are right in front of our nose. Don't get me wrong, having goals and aiming for success are fantastic, and they have their place, but I've learned that not neglecting and actually building human connections are more important than anything money could buy.

What I wouldn't give for more time to visit with my parents, my aunt and others I've lost now. Not to be too busy or too stressed to take the time to make a call or plan a visit. Not because I have too, but because I want too. To go back and be in the present moment more, enjoy their company and not take for granted that our relationship would never end.

How special it was to create our bond with our children in their young years that stands the test of time today. The gift of watching them grow and really breathing in each milestone without distraction. Knowing the moments are fleeting. Making the most of each day the best we can. A constant reminder that this time in life won't happen again and to savor each minute. It's the same energy we should also apply to our friendships.

How many friendships do you have where although you love those friends to pieces, don't give adequate time, too?

The actions of others resonate with me much more than any words spoken. People can tell you many things, but are they showing you with their actions? Actions that equal or surpass spoken words are how relationships strengthen, in my opinion. By far this is one of my biggest takeaways learned throughout our ordeal. I make it a point to reach out and show those dear to me what they mean to me. Showing others how you feel about them and having it returned is priceless. This way, there's never a question that you mean what you say. Reciprocation is the key, though; otherwise it's energy wasted.

I cannot express how difficult it was to experience being alone amidst our tough times. How much the kindness of one person became the strength I needed to make it through the next moment. To appreciate someone reaching out to check on me or provide words of comfort or encouragement. It made such an impact on me.

I vowed from that moment to always let those close to me know how much they mean, through good times or bad. Little things make all the difference. Taking time out of a busy schedule to send a text, a note or make a call. Plan a walk together. Make a plan to meet for coffee, take a photo together or escape and see a movie. Say "yes" to that invitation and reach out to others to include them in your life. Small actions to show you're listening, thinking of them and care about building the relationship.

Maybe it's date night with your spouse or significant other, a special time set aside with your kiddos, or even a hug, smile or compliment to brighten a day. Cook a meal, gather for a game night—the ideas are endless.

I'm not perfect at it, but I'm working on it each day and taking action! I'm hoping when I leave this earth one day, that I'm able to have at touched enough lives where at least one person says, "she made a difference in my life".

We've been fortunate enough to live a life some people only dream about. We've also been unfortunate enough to experience great loss. It opened our eyes. Especially because we are getting older. No matter how much I try to deny it, health becomes a natural changing obstacle. We choose to never again work ourselves to the bone. Even with multiple businesses and interests, we've designed our life to be manageable between us. The minute things get too busy, we re-evaluate and remove the overwhelm. We find ways to work smarter, not longer, manage stress and spend more time with family and friends.

You've heard of the adage, "When life gives you lemons, you make lemonade." The recipe for making that lemonade, in this example, is your toolkit. It's all about your outlook on life. The choices you make throughout each day, week, month to take care of yourself and not lose hope!

Let's take a look at Part Two. The Survivor's Toolkit. I put together the tools I found most useful in helping us survive our own personal storm. Tools I've since developed that I wish I knew about during the most difficult moments of our storm. I've created this toolkit just for you. It is my hope that it can help you weather any storm that may come your way.

PART II
The Survivor's Toolkit

PART II

The Surgeon's Toolkit

NINE

The Survivor's Toolkit

When we were going through our own personal storm, many times I had wished someone could hold my hand and tell me everything would be ok. I also wished that someone who had been through it before could guide me. My husband and I just had each other, which thankfully was enough. It's normal to feel alone and inadequate through life's storms. That's why you need the right tools.

Whether you are currently riding out a storm, have been through one in your life, or anticipate one in the future, you need what I call the Survivor's Toolkit. It contains the tools you need to get through the hard times that will inevitably come your way. Just like you would gather food, water, or other items in preparation for a bad storm, you need to have these tools ready so you can get through hard times better.

In this section, I'm going to teach you how to get through your own personal storm. Creating and implementing these useful habits when life is calm, helps to maintain healthy habits when it's not. You don't need a to wait for a storm to brew to be healthy. Here are the four main tools you need:

- **Tool #1: Awareness and Perspective**
- **Tool #2: Passions**
- **Tool #3: Time Management**
- **Tool #4: Self-care**

You don't have to collect all of these tools at once, but the more you choose collect and keep in your toolkit, the better you'll feel – I promise! Begin by picking one small change and work on it wholly and completely before moving onto the next. My suggestion is to find what resonates with you! Below, I'll outline the steps necessary to take action so you can make effective change and create the life you want.

Tool #1: Awareness and Perspective

Your mind can take you to dark places if you let it. I chose to not allow my mind to take me there in our darkest time. I began researching helpful tools and developed an amazing exercise for myself. It helped me change negative thoughts, recognizing and dismissing them as they arrived. I know it will help you, too.

For every negative thought that enters your mind, combat it with a positive one! We can "what if" ourselves to death:

"What if I lose my job?"

"What if I'm too scared to __?"

But, "what if" every time a negative thought popped into our brains, we countered it with a positive one?

"What if I succeed?"

"What if I got the job of my dreams?"

Even the simple, "What if it doesn't happen" is effective against the worry of "What might happen"!

I found this quote and put it up on my computer screensaver so I could see it each day at work as a reminder. It helped change my outlook on life. Perhaps you've heard of it before?

"Life is 10% what happens to us and 90% how we REACT to it!"

It struck a chord with me. From that day on, I focused on my perspective. I focused on when I was reacting and consciously calmed myself down. I searched for the actual reality of the situation, instead of the negative scary thought. I developed a mindset advantage!

It's a lot of work being aware of thoughts that pass through the mind. We think negative thoughts any given second, minute or hour. According to the article, "Change Your Thoughts, Change Your World" on www.jenniferhawthorne.com, researchers estimate we humans think up to 12,000 to 60,000 thoughts per day, with 98% repeated from the day before.

Some research has even suggested 80% of our thoughts are negative. Eighty percent! Incredible, huh? So what can we do to keep our minds focused on the positive? Be consistent in recognizing the negative thoughts and pay attention and mindful to counter with positive thoughts. Don't accept the negative! If our thoughts repeat daily, wouldn't it be better to have the positive ones on replay?

Below I outline seven things that helped me most. I encourage you to test them out.

1. Write it Down

Write down all negative thoughts that come to mind. Immediately counter them with positive thoughts. Keep a pen and paper close or use the note app on your phone and jot them down, one by one. Think of an opposing positive thought to negate each one.

Continue until this process becomes an easier, recognizable, quick mental correction. The list will grow within minutes. Don't be afraid how fast they stack up. Just go with it. With time and practice, a change will happen, along with the ability to distinguish the negative, untrue thoughts.

I created a worksheet for myself to track my own negative thinking. It really helped me become aware of my own bad habit!

2. Stay Positive

Don't let others' negativity bring you down. It will be easy to begin to recognize the negativity in others as you become more self-aware. For fun, you can even try silently countering their negative thoughts with a positive reply.

3. Let Go of the Negative

Begin to find the best of each situation and build from it. Continuing to think in negative patterns doesn't help you feel better. Nor does it help you bring change to your thought process. Keep negativity out of your life. This includes people or situations that don't better serve you.

4. Look for the Good

Look for things that inspire. I like daily inspirational quotes, quotes from the Bible, the universe or other positive messages. Whatever's needed to help keep your focus. Start your day with a positive affirmation or keep that inspirational message close at hand to remind you throughout the day that better times are ahead.

. . .

5. Meditate

Download my free calming mediation and get started (michelelaine.com/resource-toolkit). We aren't trying to stop thoughts from happening when meditating. We want to focus on our breathing as we bring ourselves back to the present moment. Allow the thoughts to float in and out, bringing your focus back to the breath. Meditation brings much calming relief to an anxious mind. It's available to use as often as needed throughout the day. I even enjoy using the sleep meditations as a great way to relax into deep sleep.

6. Be Present

Stay in the moment as much as possible. Be happy where you are now. Be present—don't live in the past or worry about the future. Even while making changes, you can appreciate each moment. It takes practice, but begin by paying attention to wandering thoughts. Do your best to focus on the place you're in and the people you're with. Enjoy your time in the now. Don't allow wandering, negative thoughts and worry to waste away those precious moments. Take action: get involved in the conversation, engage and be in that moment.

7. Be Grateful

Appreciate what you have instead of what you don't have and let gratitude take hold. Be mindful and grateful instead of bitter and negative. It can lift your spirits and keep your thought process on task.

Start a gratitude journal. A journal to write down all the things you are grateful for. This is helpful in recognizing all that is good in the world, especially if those things are hard to see. Write down three things each morning you are grateful for and add to the list each day (or grab my Gratitude Card Deck at michelelaine.com) Review it often!

Tool #2: Passions

What brings you happiness and intense joy? Do you have any hobbies? Have you made time for any? (FYI, your hobbies are not your kid's hobbies.) Having hobbies and passions can be a great way to find happiness. Especially if your day consists of all work and no play. It's important to have something you look forward to doing in your spare time. It's equally important to do something besides work!

Your hobbies or passions should be something that lifts your energies and puts a smile on your face. The kind of hobby or passion that inspires and drives you to your practice. Dig deep here. I'm sure there's a little voice in the back of your mind screaming out something you have interest in. As you are reading this now, what do you hear? What are you passionate about? What makes you, well, *you*? Trust what's being whispered to you.

You do NOT have to be good at this thing. You just have to be interested in it and/or love doing it. It must bring you joy in its purest form. How about a dance class, swimming, outdoor recreation, game night, hiking, or mountain biking? The list is endless; so what is it that feeds your soul? I believe everyone has something that makes them feel alive. The "thing" is different for us all, but the main difference between making it a hobby or passion is taking action and committing. Nurture that thing that makes you happy until it becomes a part of you. It will give you something to look forward to.

My most passionate hobby is dance; I began dancing at the age of 3. Being in a dance room surrounded by the smell of sweat, leather shoes and wood flooring warms my heart. The familiar wall of mirrors, ballet barres, and pumping sound system spark creativity. It's a place of self expression and excitement for me. That room provides an outlet that warms my heart and feeds my soul beyond anything else. I continued with dance through college, graduating with a teaching degree in dance. I even take part in classes and performances today! I'm not the best dancer out there, or even a professional. But that doesn't matter, because I don't dance for anyone else. I dance for me. It makes me forget everything else. It makes me feel alive.

How fortunate I've been to spend so many hundreds of hours of my life in that wonderful space. That familiar, comfortable, enchanting space. A universal space, no matter what town or studio I travel to. I look for ways to celebrate my love of dance. I make the time and continue to challenge myself. Years of dedication, hard work, and commitment. A place I first learned to face fears, let go and trust myself. All priceless experiences that I carry into all aspects of my life today.

Writing is another passion of mine. Spending time putting my thoughts to paper feeds my soul. Allowing myself this other creative outlet challenges me to communicate my thoughts. To learn to express them in a clear, concise way and allow myself the vulnerability to be a writer.

When I'm writing, I lose all sense of time. It's peaceful and enjoyable to me to bring together words on paper, formulating them into a final piece of work. It surprises me every time how fast minutes and hours fly by. Even better is knowing when I've written something that has resonated with others. It's elating and a confidence booster for my new found art.

Distractions are helpful when going through a storm. Hobbies and passions are some of the best distractions out there. But there are other things, too: time with friends, movies, music, events, school functions, your kid's activities, workouts, books. Anything to pull you into the present moment and help stop the mind from focusing on the problem at hand.

Remember when the *Twilight* series was all the rage? The author, Stephenie Meyer, transported readers to Forks, Washington. There we lived the adventures of the charming, captivating character's life in her storyline. Team Jacob (wolf) or Team Edward (vampire), anyone? Why am I referencing this delicious, iconic flashback? Because I was hook, line and sinker involved in the story line during the years of our storm. It couldn't have been a better distraction for me at that time in my life.

I was so excited each day when it came time to read my new found books. Transporting myself to a place different from the world I lived in. The first and second movies had already been in the theaters. The third installment, *Eclipse,* was ready to release. Although the movie did not compare to the books, in my opinion, I was grateful for any and all things *Twilight.* I loved them nonetheless. Anything related to this wonderful new distraction filled my free time. It helped me sleep after an hour or two of reading each night and gave me something new to look forward to daily. I was in the moment, I was present and I was completely transported to a different reality reading or watching those stories. I cannot recommend finding an outlet for yourself enough—whatever the "it" may be for you.

Let's identify your passions and outlets:

What makes you happy?

What brings you intense joy?

Jot down a list. Let yourself free write for one minute and write down all the things that pop into your mind.

Now, look at your list. How many of those things do you do on a daily or weekly basis? Any? None? Just pick one from the list to start, **choose** to make the time to make it happen and pursue it with passion.

Figure out something that takes your mind off of your current situation. It should be something that makes you feel emotions of happiness, excitement or joy. Something you look forward to each day.

Choose to take action and do those things you love most and do them often. Fill your life with joy and explore who you are through your passions.

Acknowledge the outlets available. Allow yourself to feel better and break the cycle of the pain the turmoil of the storm has added to your life.

Tool #3: Time Management

I'm often asked how I do all the things I do and still have time for me. What I'm about to share with you is my biggest secret: ready? It's **choice!** I've become a master of choosing for myself. I choose my work schedule by being self-employed. I choose how busy I allow myself to be. I transport my kids to school and their activities every day because they are only little for such a short time. I want to enjoy this crazy time with them.

I choose to make time in my schedule to meet up with a close friend for coffee, a meal, or a workout many times a week. I choose to make time to cook fresh food for my family. To take a daily walk for the betterment of my health. I choose to focus on my sleep so I can be the best, healthiest version of myself for my family and those around me.

I love helping people realize their potential. I choose to stretch my skills to see where I can take my dream of writing. I choose to find my happiness daily, to push the negative out of my head and find something better to focus on.

I choose to focus on positive self talk and encouragement, so I can be my own best cheerleader. I choose to challenge myself with learning new things in areas I'm not familiar with so I can continue to grow as a person. I choose to set new goals for myself and work toward them.

I choose. I make it happen—every day! I work toward my dream, or dream a new dream and do something toward that dream each day. It's that simple. Be consistent and make a daily habit of spending time toward your goal, your passion. Before you know it, the change will be a part of your life.

Any new habit is created within an average of 21 days of consistency and embodied within 64 days. Point being, make the *choice* to commit to make changes in your life and be consistent with your efforts. You'll reap the benefits of creating new habits within a few weeks. Great habits that get you closer to your end goals.

"If it's important to you, you'll do it, if not, you'll find an excuse." I read that quote one day and so agree! Isn't it true?

We have more excuses at the drop of a hat these days. "I'm too busy," "I'm too old," "I don't even know what I'd do with free time," "I can't workout, because my ___ hurts." You can make up excuses all day long. But the truth is, we all have the same 24 hours in a day. If you tell yourself you can't, then you can't. Likewise, if you tell yourself you can, then you can!

Let's take a look at ways to develop good time management:

1. Commit

Be consistent and book *your* time into your calendar as you would for a meeting at work, or for an appointment or an activity for your kids. Create a new habit with your consistency.

Remember to manage time for relaxation and self-care, too.

2. Say No

Say "no" to extra obligations! I've become good at saying "no" to the hundreds of obligations asked of me. Saying "no" to all those "shoulds" that would otherwise steal my focus. Choose only those obligations that make sense for your life and busy schedule. Be mindful NOT to give up the time you've carved out for your hobby or passion!

Don't feel bad about being discerning about your time. I know that sounds harsh. Imagine if we went around saying "yes" to everything asked of us and never choosing to say "no." We'd be running around in circles, like a chicken with its head cut off. We'd be exhausted and unfulfilled in life. Saying "no" is self preservation. We have minds of our own and are free to choose what works for us without being a slave to the requests of others.

3. Make Changes

What small change can you start today to move forward toward your dream or goal? For instance, how much time are you spending on social media? Is it possible you can drop 30 minutes or more and put that time toward your goal or hobby? Can you wake up a little earlier each morning to spend time toward your goal? How much television do you watch? Can you cut back an hour or two in the evening?

Don't let money be an excuse. Need a little extra money to start? How about a yard sale? Or saving money with a budget of your income and expenses? Or maybe clip coupons or no eating out? Take all that cash and set it aside for your future needs. Maybe even get a second part-time job or a loan, depending upon the amount of money needed? Life is full of possibilities; it just takes a bit of focus and opening your eyes to opportunities.

Make a plan, set your goal, decide to get to work and take action. Change your mind and change it again until your life resembles what you envision. Don't be afraid of making mistakes. We learn much more from our mistakes than we do our successes.

You can lose all your money. Money can be made, but if you lose your time, you'll never get it back. So, what's your time worth to you? What will you do with the time you have on this earth? Will you leave a legacy and inspire others? More so, what will you remember of your own life?

Do you live life to the fullest, follow your dreams and reach for the stars? My hope is that you do. If you haven't yet, it's not too late to start.

Carl Bard said: "Though no one can go back and make a brand new start, anyone can start from now and make a brand new ending."

That quote is true for me! I intend to make a new ending and not let my past defeats define me. Everyone's journey is a different one. We are individuals with differing dreams, perspectives, achievements and circumstances. That's what makes each of us unique and beautiful. Take care to carve out time in your schedule and take care of yourself. Spend time reaching your goals. It's not only satisfying, but necessary for success!

Tool #4: Self-Care

I would be remiss if I didn't touch on the most important aspect of surviving any of life's storms. None of the aforementioned tools would be nearly as valuable without adequate self-care. Self-care in its simplest form encompasses these four pillars:

1. **Managing Stress**
2. **Exercise**
3. **Nutrition**
4. **Adequate Sleep**

Let's take a look at each of these in more detail.

1. Managing Stress

Stress can sometimes be crippling, and we have to learn to manage it so it doesn't take over. Managing stress can be done in several ways.

Although it would be years later that I would learn the health benefits of meditation, I discovered a form of it during my hard years of loss. I actually found a place of peaceful recluse in my shower. I discovered the benefit of focusing on my breath by accident.

Focusing on the white noise of the shower water, as it rained down on me, brought calm to my racing thoughts and fragile emotions. Sitting on the shower floor and having my head under the water brought me peace. It shut out everything else in my world for a small time. I would take a deep breath and then another, listening to the rhythm of the water dancing on my head and feeling the warm cascading droplets run down my face. I stayed there until I was ready to face my day.

I allowed thoughts to drift in and out of my mind. I would bring back focus to the calming white noise of the shower water bouncing off surfaces. It brought me such peace through the sorrow and pain I was going through.

Regular meditation practice can do the same. Meditation is the practice of calming the mind and allowing thoughts to drift in and out. Bringing the mind back to the present moment while focusing on deep, relaxing breaths. Breathing in, breathing out. It helped me so much to manage stress in that moment, and then later when stress would creep in.

At the worst of it, each morning, it was hard to get out of bed. But I had a choice. A choice to stay curled up in a ball, blocking out the world and allowing my stress and sorrow to consume me. Or I could choose to wake up and tell myself to pull myself together. Luckily, I chose the latter. I forced myself to get up, get in and out of the shower, get dressed, dry and style my hair and put my makeup on. Just doing that each day also helped to manage my stress.

I made sure I kept my nails done. I loved to glance at them during the day, watching as they danced along the keyboard. It was important to me to maintain a sense of self through the days when it felt I was stripped of my dignity and self worth. The sight of my nails manicured reminded me to not give up hope and stay the course. It brought me joy in the most simplistic form during a stressful time. Little victories.

Making myself get ready each day gave me strength to work through the emotions and fear. A chance to remind myself that our situation may be our new normal now, but it wouldn't be forever. No matter how long it felt like it would be. Life just doesn't work that way. Life goes on. We had to work through to make it to the other side. Getting up each day and getting ready was a way to work through it for me.

Walking daily was also a tremendous help in mitigating stress. Walking helped calm my nerves and anxious mind when I needed it most and continued to sooth my soul as time passed. Walking helped me organize my thoughts and keep that clarity. It helped to create a sense of peace and focus to gain perspective on reality vs fear.

I found it useful having a mantra when walking to remind myself of better times ahead. One mantra I used often was, "This too shall pass." I also liked, "One day we'll have this all behind us." It was a helpful practice to just take time to open my eyes and look around at life going by while I was walking.

The cars with drivers heading to and fro. Kids on their bikes, families outside, birds singing, dogs on walks. The beautiful leaves on the trees, the changing seasonal flowers and the sun on my shoulders. I would take a deep breath and fill my lungs with clean, fresh air, then exhale. Repeat and keep walking. Today, I still enjoy the benefits of walking. The hormonal reset that happens with a long walk. The peaceful "me" time. The beauty of my surroundings and the health benefits of being outdoors.

2. Exercise

Stress is a silent killer. My husband and I could feel the toll it was taking on us each day as we dealt with the closing of our business and the losses in our family. A heaviness like none other. One big stress reliever for us was hitting the gym. Exercise was my much needed, anticipated hour of normalcy. A chance to be among like minded people and another chance to not think about anything else in my world at that moment.

Just lifting weights and working on my strength and conditioning.

It was my stress relief, my moments of strength in an uncertain, broken world. Being in the gym inspired me to become the best physical version of myself. To set new goals for myself. I'm quite certain my workouts were my saving grace during our stressful time. I'm not sure where'd I be today if I hadn't keep up with it.

I love weights and their effect on the entire body. With a background in dance, body awareness is second nature to me. Weightlifting was a natural transition in learning correct placement and great lifting form. I had no idea what I was capable of. Embracing strength, staying the course and pushing beyond personal limits brought tremendous results mentally and physically. I felt confident in myself and found determination to continue in every area of my life. It was a welcome relief from the day to day impact of our collapsing world.

Money was tight. I was always so appreciative to have the ability to continue at my gym; I never took one day for granted. I will never forget the generosity of gym management accommodating me at that time. I would not be who I am today without their help and compassion.

So let's summarize the ways to manage stress:

- *Meditate*

Meditate daily, even if it's only one to three minutes. Again, getting into a daily habit of setting aside time to meditate will make it second nature in a few short weeks. Once you're used to the practice of meditation and the calm it brings the mind, you'll appreciate it more. You'll desire the recluse. You may even wonder how you ever lived without it!

- *Walk*

Walk as much as you can, as often as you can. Get outside and pay attention to the beauty that surrounds you. Grab a buddy to walk with you, even if that buddy is your furry friend. Our pets need the exercise as much as we do! Be mindful of using walking mantras to help set you on a positive path and keep perspective straight.

- *Exercise*

Lift heavy things and get some exercise. Move some weights. Find a gym with a trainer who can coach you on safe, sound technique and incorporate functional movements. There needs to be a balance when exercising under stress.

If you find yourself working out even when you are overly stressed or exhausted, it could be counterproductive to over train in an effort to manage your stress. I now know that I should have backed off a bit on working out instead of relying on exercise as a tool to "power me through." A gentle approach would have been kindler on my adrenals at that time.

Pay attention to how you're feeling. Some days a few heavy lifts and lots of walking can be the best way to manage stress until life mellows out. The harder workouts will be there for you as you heal. Set goals for your success, be consistent and train smart. You'll witness benefits first hand in no time.

- *Breathe*

Breathe! Something so simple that we take for granted can be a useful tool in reducing stress levels. Many times a day, take a few moments to breathe in deep and exhale through your nose. Place your tongue at the roof of your mouth and keep it in place while breathing in and out. Breathe in for a count of four and exhale for a count of eight.

Open that airway to breathe deep into the belly following with a steady exhale through the nose. Try your best to avoid short breathing into your chest—I'm talking large, deep breaths here!

Notice how much better you feel after just three breaths. Work your way up to six to eight deep breaths, many times a day. Especially when feeling anxious.

Repeat as often as needed.

- *Bath*

Bonus tip. Take a warm, relaxing Epsom salt and lavender oil bath in the evenings if accessible. The therapy of warm water and lavender does wonders for the body, melting stress away. The Epsom salt relieves sore muscles and rids toxins from the body. Lavender oil calms and relaxes. Both items can easily be found at your local health store or online at Amazon.com. Light some candles, add a bath pillow, relax for 15-20 minutes and melt the day away.

Be consistent and diligent with self-care to experience the benefits of stress reduction.

Even by choosing only one or two of these options above, you'll experience the benefits of managing stress with conscious effort. Image how you'd feel incorporating them all.

3. Nutrition

Eating good, clean food is essential and something my husband and I believe in. Through our storm, cooking became a passion of mine. I desired to provide healthy, nutritious meals in our household. With the help of the Food Network and a variety of cookbooks, I taught myself how to cook. My husband is a phenomenal cook. It was fun spending time finally cooking healthy meals together and getting the kids involved. It became our family event, teaching valuable life skills on self reliance and independence.

I had been following a Paleo lifestyle at that time, as introduced to me at my gym. It was during this time of cooking that I also discovered a website called Everyday Paleo. Inspired by the author, Sarah Fragoso, I was ready to make changes for our family, too. I gobbled up as many recipes as I could because my family loved the food. Simple ingredients and real food, free from preservatives. So delicious and healthy! Having new found skills, I got better and better at cooking great food.

Her message of creating real, simple, delicious food fast and easy, getting adequate sleep, training smart and managing stress inspired me.

It's funny what life throws at you and how life can round full circle. I knew of Sarah from my gym. Her husband, John, was my chiropractor for years. But Sarah and I never had the chance to get to really get to know each other well until later years. The longer I live, the more I believe there are no accidents in life.

Here's what you can do to improve your nutrition:

- *Variety*

Eat a variety of delicious, clean food. Fuel your body with healthy carbohydrates as needed for your levels of exercise. Focus on eating fruits, vegetables, meats. Add healthy fats like extra virgin olive oil, avocado, coconut oil, ghee and nuts into your diet.

- *Gluten*

Avoid gluten which is found in wheat, including all wheat varieties such as spelt, kamut, faro and durum, and other grains such as barley, rye, and oats dependent on how the oats have been processed. Gluten can cause inflammation in the gut, even for those who aren't celiac or gluten intolerant, and this can lead to a myriad of health problems. To help lower inflammation, consider trying gluten free foods as substitutions. Avoid all grains altogether if you notice they're problematic for you. But if you are able to tolerate some grains, enjoy the occasional corn tortilla or white rice, which are inherently gluten free. You can also substitute potatoes, sweet potatoes, and winter squash as more nutritionally dense starch choices.

- *Dairy*

If you choose to eat dairy, look for grass fed and whole fat dairy products. Try to avoid processed low fat or fat free dairy products with added sugars and hormones.

- *Don't Skip*

Don't skip meals. Maintaining level blood sugar is key to avoid cravings and overeating later in the day. Plus, you want to keep your metabolism humming on all cylinders. Starving the body too much will lead to blood sugar highs and lows and will affect your metabolism negatively. When your metabolism slows or shuts down, the body has a hard time keeping extra pounds away. Especially during times of stress! It's a vicious cycle.

- *Portions*

Maintain healthy portion control at meals. Protein should be roughly the length and thickness of your palm. Fill the rest of your plate with veggies, and use healthy fats. Add a small amount of carbohydrates from the list above on weight lifting days.

- *Sugar*

Avoid sugar. Be mindful of the use of sugar in products such as ketchup, sauces, dressings, etc. Sugar is addictive and empty of nutrients. It's much easier to maintain stable blood sugar and mood by removing this temptation from your diet.

- *Alcohol*

Avoid excess alcohol. Alcohol turns to sugar in the body and sugar is sugar. It's easy to grab an extra glass of wine or two during stressful times, but you have the tools of mindfulness and meditation to help you with this now. Numbing your feelings with alcohol is avoidance. It can lead to further problems if left unchecked.

- *Food Prep*

Take care of food preparation once each week. Cook meals ahead of time and freeze portions for the week ahead. This way all you have to do is defrost one from the freezer when you're pressed for time. We like to do this on Sundays so we have a head start for our week.

Making use of your crock pot is another great way to have a meal ready at the end of a busy day. A little advanced prep the night before or morning of, the use of timer settings on the crock pot and dinner is served when you walk in the door. Cook up some beef, chicken or pork with lots of yummy seasonings and shred the finished product. You'll have plenty of leftover meat for tacos, salads, or snacks from one pot!

- *Shop Smart*

Shop from the outside perimeter of the grocery store. The inner isles of the store are full of cake mix, cereal, pasta, desserts, chips, processed and sugary foods. Avoid those temptations. Replace them with healthy meats, nuts and veggies instead.

- *Shop Local*

Locate a local CSA (community-supported agriculture) or Farmer's Market in or around your community. This is a great source for seasonal fresh vegetables and fruit. It's important to know now where your food comes from. What's better than fresh, locally grown produce? Using a CSA or local Farmer's Market for your fruits and veggies also supports local farms. If you are lucky enough to have one in your area, you can feel good about knowing more about your food source before it hits your table.

- *Cook at Home*

Eat at home as often as possible. Be mindful of hidden ingredients, including vegetable oils, gluten, or other allergens when eating out. Ask about food preparation and don't be afraid to request substitutions.

4. Adequate Sleep

Sleep is the final component in our Survivor's Toolkit. In my opinion, it's the most important thing you can do to improve health. I'll admit, I had to learn this information the hard way. That alone makes me so excited to be able to share it with you, so you don't have to suffer as I did.

Sleep was the first thing I gave up to make room to do more in my day. When the kids were young, after they'd gone to sleep, I'd stay up late. It was my chance to finally watch some TV, read and have some "me" time without kids present. Sleep was also the one place I could reduce to create more time to catch up on work I didn't finish in my day. There was always more work to do.

Once our storm hit, my body was overrun with stress. It was not only difficult to fall asleep, but stay asleep through the night. That pattern continued long enough to become a bad habit to break. I had no idea at the time the effects lack of sleep had on the human body.

According to Healthy Sleep (a resource from the division of Sleep Medicine at Harvard Medical School's website), there are consequences to insufficient sleep.

> *"In the short term, a lack of adequate sleep can affect judgment, mood, ability to learn and retain information, and may increase the risk of serious accidents and injury. In the long term, chronic sleep deprivation may lead to a host of health problems including*

obesity, diabetes, cardiovascular disease, and even early mortality."

Until I experienced my own health problems, I never considered the value of a good night's sleep. Of course I felt tired when I hadn't had adequate sleep, but I never knew the further effects on my body. Believe it or not, hormone changes affect sleep as well. I found myself stuck in a perpetual cycle of insufficient sleep, an abundance of stress and wonky hormones! Things needed to change.

I researched better sleep quality and applied what I learned. I learned the value of a dark, cool room to sleep in. Getting rid of blue lights in the room and creating a consistent bedtime routine. I aimed for at least eight hours of sleep a night and going to bed at the same time each night.

These things help us reset our natural circadian rhythm. What's our circadian rhythm, you ask? It's our bodies' natural 24-hour wake and sleep cycle. Allowing us to sleep when it's dark and wake when it's light outside.

Have you ever noticed when sitting around a campfire, the orange glow of the fire begins to make you sleepy? You go to bed shortly after dark and wake refreshed at dawn when camping. This is no accident; it's your body responding to its natural circadian rhythm cycle. It's key for a good night's sleep.

What was the result of implementing these sleep changes? My health began to improve once I got more sleep! My cortisol (stress) levels stabilized. I fell asleep faster and slept longer and sounder. I began to guard my sleep like never before and created improved sleep habits in return.

Although my sleep is not perfect every night, it's a huge improvement from five years ago. I have the tools needed to ensure I give myself the best chance possible for a good night's rest each night. As with other components of my self-care, I've chosen to make sleep one of my top priorities.

I'm going to share with you the tips I've learned so you have the opportunity to improve your sleep, too. It's worth testing them out to see what improvements you can make in your own sleep hygiene. Pay attention to how much better you feel with a little more rest.

Here are ways you, too, can reset your circadian rhythm at home:

- *Screens*

About an hour or two before bedtime, shut down any electronic screens such as the television, computer or smartphones. This will help your brain wind down before bed.

Research shows the emitted blue and white light from electronic devices send signals to the brain that it's still daylight outside. This light prevents our own production of melatonin and disrupts our circadian rhythm, which are both needed for a restful night's sleep.

- *Lights*

Dim the lights throughout the house, or substitute orange bulbs or candle light after sunset. This will assist your brain in stimulating melatonin production and prepare to sleep. Since the invention of the light bulb, we are able to light up our world 24 hours a day, but this advancement has unfortunately fooled our brains into thinking it's daytime all the time.

Make sure your room is cool and pitch black. Cover the glow of a cable box light and clock so the blue light isn't interfering with your sleep. Invest in blackout curtains or find a way to make the room completely dark at night. Avoid letting moonlight or outside street lighting into your room. If that's not a workable solution, you can do what I do and use a light blocking sleep mask. A variety of masks are found online. You may have to experiment with a few styles to find your favorite fit.

- *Same Time*

Go to bed roughly at the same time each night and get as many hours of sleep before midnight as possible. This will increase your Human Growth Hormone (HGH) production. HGH production is highest in our sleep cycle after we first fall asleep and before the hour of midnight. HGH repairs the body during sleep. As we age, we produce less. Something as simple as going to sleep a little earlier each day helps our bodies restore and replenish during the night. What better reason to make this change?

Eight hours of sleep between the hours of 10:00pm and 6:00am, as an example, will leave you much more rested than eight hours of sleep after staying up later.

- *Eight Hours*

Go to sleep early enough that you can wake without an alarm. Aim for at least eight hours of sleep each night. If upon waking you're still tired, you need more sleep. Adequate sleep will leave you waking refreshed and ready to tackle the day. Try moving your bedtime back 15 minutes until you find a time more conducive to waking rested.

- *Outside*

Get outside as often as you can throughout the day to help reset your body's circadian rhythm. Take a stroll at sunset or step outside in the evening. Look to the sun upon waking. This will help reset your natural circadian rhythms through sunset and sunrise natural lighting.

- *Caffeine*

Avoid caffeine after 1 p.m. Caffeine stays in our system six to eight hours after consumption. It can impact our ability to fall and stay asleep. Even alcohol can impair your ability to get a restful night's sleep; another thing to be mindful of.

- *Breathe*

Take five to seven deep breaths before bedtime as described in the *Managing Stress* tool. Deep breathing helps lower cortisol levels and relaxes the body in preparation for sleep.

Nothing replaces a good night's sleep for feeling like a million bucks. It's also your best beauty secret, your best body healer, productivity provider and fat loss optimizer. Lack of sleep can derail your best efforts in eating right and exercising, too. You owe it to yourself to get the best quality of sleep possible. Your body will thank you.

My philosophy is, self-care shouldn't be a want—it should be a need. A necessity. Something we practice daily. When we care for ourselves first, we are better able to care for others. Not the other way around.

Managing stress, exercise, good nutrition and adequate sleep —the four pillars of health—can make all the difference in your body and mind. Your approach to life. Make these tools a part of your lifestyle and they won't seem like work. They'll become second nature and a healthy way of life. When the storms roll in, you'll have the strength to keep thriving.

So, now you too have my four proven strategies (tools) in your Survivor's Toolkit to survive any storm. **Awareness and perspective** to keep your head high, turn negative thoughts to powerful positive thoughts and the right perspective to get you through your storm.

Identify your **passions** to spend time doing whatever it is that makes you feel alive. Something you look forward to and that grounds you during the storm.

Manage your time and schedule your calendar to include time for your passions, your friends and the things that matter most in life. Work toward your goals and dreams to make them a reality. Say "no" to extra obligations that don't work for you.

And finally, **take care of yourself.** Living with a high amount of stress has negative repercussions. Become better at making self-care a priority in your life. Notice the strength gained from taking care of yourself. Live a healthy lifestyle to be the most vibrant you!

Storms may come, but you don't have to fear them. Have courage, develop these tools in your toolkit, and you'll be stronger than any storm that comes your way.

TEN

After the Storm

Have you ever noticed how beautiful the morning is after the storm? Everything feels fresh and clean, the sun shines a bit brighter and the sky is clear and blue.

When the gloomy clouds are gone, there may be evidence left behind of the storm. Fallen leaves, broken branches or debris on the ground from the day before, but the day after is bright and full of promise. That describes us after a storm. We may be battered and bruised from the journey, but bright and full of promise from coming through the storm.

Even though things are better now, I am sure more storms will come our way again. They will come your way, too.

Will there be bumps along the way? Sure. Will everything be perfect? Of course not, but that's where the Survivor's Toolkit comes in handy. It's not about avoiding the storms of life, but arming yourself with tools to make it through. To face the hurricane and come out of it even stronger than before.

Be stronger than the storm!

After all, we learn much more from living through our adversities in life. Enjoy these tools after the storm has passed and continue onto a path of healthy living.

In every aspect of life, we have choices!

It's choices that take us to the next decision—the next choice. My hope is you choose to care for yourself and become the best version of yourself possible. Don't let the storms of life beat you down—find a way to keep going and survive. We all have more inner strength within us than we realize!

It's important to spend some time getting to know who you are. Make time each day to live true to yourself and not become complacent or comfortable. Plan a life full of love, friendship, happiness, dreams, adventures and memories. Be bold and confident. Bright and alluring. Intelligent and gracious, and above all, do not be afraid to take risks or face fears. It's by doing so that we learn the best of ourselves and reach our fullest potential.

It's guaranteed that life provides surprises. Don't wait for life to pass you by or think that you can start making changes "tomorrow." Tomorrow may never come. Or maybe tomorrow will be followed with a huge unexpected storm of life that will change your path.

We have only one chance to make every day count and make our dreams a reality. One lifetime to rise above any challenge and learn from our experiences. Through our failures, our trials of life, we build resilience, perseverance and strength. The key is to allow those failures to build you, not break you.

I don't want you to live with regret. Life is too short! Join me on my quest of self-discovery. Make choices, make decisions and create the life you want, before the years pass you by. Take care of your health and never stop learning. Absolutely, positively, never, ever give up on yourself in the process. We are the difference makers with the power of choice. Keep reaching, searching and working to find your most authentic self. You're in there, I promise.

Thank you for reading my book. You now know too much to let setbacks or storms in life break you. You have the knowledge and tools necessary to allow the change you desire. I've shared with you first hand that it can be done. I leave you with this last thought . . . you are never too old to make life changes. Life's meant to be lived to the fullest every minute we're on this earth. So what are you waiting for?

Take action; the life you've always dreamed of awaits!

THE GRATITUDE SHIFT

64-Gratitude Guidance Cards

I am grateful for...

paying forward my abundance
with my love, energy, time,
compassion, and money

I am grateful for...

recognizing old patterns of
thought that keep me from
living a thriving life

I am grateful f...

not being at the whim
emotions and choosi
take my dreams hig

THE GRATITUDE
SHIFT

Gratitude Guidance Cards
A 64-Card Deck

MICHELE LAINE

Available at: https://michelelaine.com

Acknowledgements

There were so many awesome people that inspired me to write this book. Each of you helped me improve it and make it possible. Thanks for your support and for helping make this book great! I could write a whole book on the amazingness of each and every one of you.

First, I have to thank my family: Scott Laine, Sami Laine and Jenna Laine. I could never have made this possible without your patience and understanding. So many hours away from you—writing, editing and processing. You never once complained about so much of my free time spent working toward my goal. For this, I'm forever grateful. Scott, your encouragement and belief in me is incomparable. You always believe in me even when I doubt myself. You're fearless and you inspire me to be stronger and fearless too. Thank you for your willingness and courage to share our crazy story.

Sarah Fragoso, you inspired my passion for writing and showed me a way to make it all possible. Your willingness to share your knowledge and honesty with me throughout this process has been priceless. You've taught me to not be afraid to reach out and share myself with others.

Rina Thoma, your endless support and encouragement provided strength whenever I needed it. Thank you for always being willing to listen and brainstorm a concept with me. I'll forever be grateful. You have a gift my friend!

Thank you to Chandler Bolt, RE Vance, Sean Sumner and team at Self-Publishing School. I'm here because of you. This system is so much more than a program. It's community, friendship and a life changing experience. Thank you for the endless information and knowledge shared to make this book a reality.

To Shawn Gower and the gang at Norcal Strength and Conditioning, thank you for being there for me during some of the toughest years of my life. Whether you knew it then or not, you helped me survive my storm every day I walked through your doors.

Dain Sandoval, without you my ability to use technology wouldn't exist. Thank you for always making me look savvy! You've been a crucial part of bringing my website, landing pages and links to life. Your patience and expertise are abundant and appreciated. What would I do without you?!!!

Lastly, to the people that made this book possible. Carrie Snider, my wonderful editor. Without you, my words would not have come to life on the page. Jennifer Sparks, you and your crazy, mad artistic skills made this book's cover beyond STUNNING! Thank you for pushing me to keep going when things were difficult and thank you for being there every step of the way!

About the Author

Michele Laine is a Conscious Self-Mastery Mentor, Intuitive Life & Business Coach, and Master Numerologist. She is an International, Best Selling Author of *Stronger Than The Storm, Proven Strategies to Conquer Fear, Discover Strength, and Overcome The Unexpected* and Creatrix of Elevate Women's Retreats.

Since publishing her first book, Michele has spent the past years studying Neuro-Transformation, Numerology, Emotional Mastery, Quantum Energy, Universal Law and has established her coaching business through Michele Laine Coaching.

She's passionate about helping people live a healthy, soul empowered life through embracing the deeper inner workings and possibilities within the mind-body connection.

Michele spends her time guiding entrepreneurs, visionary humans, and change-makers to transform their personal and professional lives through activating their purpose and embodying their personal power. She helps them remember who they are beyond the daily hustle, obligation, and overwhelm so they can claim the well-being and wealth they desire most, and experience the freedom of sustainable success when they do.

Michele believes you belong to ANY dream you desire to create for yourself. She has multiple ways to help you shift and break through the root of what's been keeping you feeling stuck and disconnected in your life. She'll help you bridge the gap by cultivating the energetic, mental, emotional, and physical mastery needed to connect those dreams down into your body, where they can be amplified and brought to life.

Michele lives in Chico, CA with her husband Scott. They have two children, Samantha and Jenna, and two goofy Boxers named Freddie and Kona.

~

Connect with Me!

Instagram:

https://www.instagram.com/coachmichelelaine_

Facebook personal page:

https://www.facebook.com/michelelaine.7

Facebook business page:

https://www.facebook.com/coachmichelelaine

Youtube:

https://www.youtube.com/
channel/UCrJLu5sloBqIZR6YfgzqmPw

Website: www.michelelaine.com

Are you feeling like you are experiencing a transition in your life? Perhaps curious what it would be like to actually have a conversation with me to find out more about your numbers? I'd love to share insightful information with you about your birth date that can bring clarity and focus after the chaos, especially during significant life-changing seasons.

Schedule your FREE 20-minute Mini Breakthrough Blueprint with me to discover how to cultivate more peace and ease in your life!

michelelainecoaching.as.me/FREE-Miniblueprint

Be a Ray of Sunshine

Would you help someone you had never met? What if you could help them in a meaningful way without it costing you a cent?

If your answer was, "Yes!" then I have an opportunity for you!

Would you be willing to help me share my story with the world?

My ask is simple.

People do judge books by the reviews left on them and reviews are a form of social proof that a book is worth a reader's time and investment. I want to share my story with the world and that will require a village of willing helpers!

One of the most helpful things you can do to help an author out is to **review their book on a bookseller's platform. Let other readers know what you loved and learned!**

If you feel so inclined, posting a picture of yourself with the book, or the cover of the book on social media with your honest review is also helpful. Of course, TAG ME!

Together, we can do great things! Thanks in advance for your support!

Thank you so much!
~Michele

Made in the USA
Las Vegas, NV
07 March 2024

86854061R00075